SEEDS SOWN

A Walk of Faith With the
Intention of Restoration

Ann E. Gustafson, RN BSN

Published by Two Penny Publishing
850 E Lime Street #266
Tarpon Springs, FL 34688
TwoPennyPublishing.com
info@twopennypublishing.com

For permission requests and ordering information, email the publisher at: info@twopennypublishing.com

"It Is Well with My Soul" Words by Horatio G. Spafford (1873). Music by Philip P. Bliss (1876). Public Domain.

Devotional excerpt taken from Live in Grace, Walk in Love by Bob Goff Copyright © 2019 by Bob Goff. Used by permission of HarperCollins Christian Publishing. www.harpercollinschristian.com

Taken from New Morning Mercies by Paul David Tripp, Copyright © 2014, pp. 140, 145-146. Used by permission of Crossway, a publishing ministry of Good News Publishers, Wheaton, IL 60187, www.crossway.org.

"I Was There to Hear Your Borning Cry." Verses 5-7. Used by permission. © 1985. John Ylvisaker, c/o Fern M. Kruger, Box 321, Waverly, Iowa 50677.

"Vintage wheat farming, farmer, agriculture logo template vector illustration design" graphic from Vecteezy.com.

"Farm field line illustration. Vector hand drawn black silhouette of wheat ears set. Bunch of grain barley. Banner design. Barley illustration in vintage style. Wheat grain, granule, kernel, oat" graphic from Vecteezy.com.

Scripture quotations marked (NIV) are taken from the Holy Bible, New International Version®, NIV®. Copyright © 1973, 1978, 1984, 2011 by Biblica, Inc.™ Used by permission of Zondervan. All rights reserved worldwide. www.zondervan.com. The "NIV" and "New International Version" are trademarks registered in the United States Patent and Trademark Office by Biblica, Inc.™

Scripture quotations marked (KJV) are taken from The Authorized (King James) Version. Rights in the Authorized Version in the United Kingdom are vested in the Crown. Reproduced by permission of the Crown's patentee, Cambridge University Press

ISBN: 978-1-950995-86-8
eBook also available

Library of Congress Control Number: 2022917204

FIRST EDITION

For more information about the author or to book her for your next event or media interview, please contact her representative at: info@twopennypublishing.com

Two Penny Publishing is a partnership publisher of a variety of genres. We help first-time and seasoned authors share their stories, passion, knowledge, and experiences that help others grow and learn. Please visit our website: TwoPennyPublishing.com if you would like us to consider your manuscript or book idea for publishing.

PRAISE FOR SEEDS SOWN

"What an incredible, insightful and important book! As a woman who has seen both family and friends battle cancer, my only wish is that I would have had this resource sooner. Ann Gustafson puts into words what so many others have felt, I'm sure, and her perspective is full of so much wisdom and hope! This is a book that will surely have an impact on so many!"

Hope Baker, Business Owner

"With courage and heart, Ann shares her health battle and through her story shows us the strength that can come from faith. Her story not only equips us with knowledge to help us with our physical health but creates a desire for us to seek a deeper restoration of all facets of our life."

Jayme Keseley, Business Owner

"Real, raw, and rewarding. Get inside the life of Ann as she trusts the process and knows the plan has been set for her with her journey through cancer. If you have been through or are going through cancer treatment of any kind and are God-fearing or not, this will bring life to your soul. I recommend everyone of faith and failure to read even if not personally affected by cancer."

Dr. Katie Layden, DC

"If you are looking for THE way to add health, love, light and healing to your journey in life, look no further. Ann has lived it, breathed it, been brave enough to write it down for you as a gentle guide into a healthier life. This book is not only the story of grit and love and transformation, it's a roadmap for you to live your best life."

Tanda Cook, ND, Naturopathic Doctor and Health Coach

"I finished it. It was so good, I couldn't stop reading it until the end."

Dad

This book is dedicated to my surgeon.

You said one sentence in my initial appointment that has been repeating in my mind and tugging on my heart since that day: *Disease doesn't follow the rules.* Thank you for humbling me and stripping my pride around my health journey. In my quest to live a healthy life, I had forgotten I wasn't entirely in control of my life, and I never will be in charge of my life—God's in charge of my life.

I am thankful to the wise mentor who taught you. I am forever grateful you shared such a poignant reminder with me that day.

The above sentence changed how I approached my surgery and my journey of conquering colon cancer. I felt unsettled after hearing you share the truth until I sat down to write this book.

Thank you for bringing clarity to my journey.
You have my utmost respect.

TABLE OF CONTENTS

FOREWORD

I'd like to introduce my younger sister, Ann Gustafson. As sisters with four years between us, we didn't become the besties that we are today until life blessed us with the same two titles: wife and mom. Our phones now text, ring or facetime often to say "good morning" or "how is your project going?" or "can you pray for me?" We are closer today living thousands of miles apart than we were when we shared "fall leaf houses" in our front yard.

Being the final granddaughter of 44 grandchildren, Ann received the well manicured qualities from our families. She was gifted with the elegance and grace of our grandma and our mom, wrapped with the love for people from our grandpa and tied with determination, hard work, and faith from our dad. Ann and I grew up with our two older brothers on a working farm in Iowa having personal chores to do, specific places to sit at the table, and rules to follow. Our rules were not written on a board for all to see—they were written in our hearts, "Love God, and love others." We were taught, in every part of our lives, to love Christ above all things.

Seeds Sown shares how faith in Jesus is planted and grows. Ann is authentic in her faith walk, proof that her faith was not just planted. She has intentionally followed the Spirit wherever she has been asked to go—even if that place includes bi-weekly chemotherapy infusions. I am humbled by her faith as we share prayer requests between one another and witness answers to our prayers; we sharpen one another as we love our husbands and kids as commanded by God; we lean into God's word together through a bible study comparing what God is teaching each of us in the same verse and chapter. Ann loves Jesus. She holds onto His goodness on the mountains and in the valleys. And Ann is not afraid to tell others about her Savior. Her faith is as noticeable as her stiletto heels on a grocery run.

Fueled by her faith my sister, Ann, loves, sees, and knows people. In *Seeds Sown*, you will encounter many names of people in Ann's life. She is genuine as she interacts with neighbors, co-workers, friends, and family. Ann is not a friend because she "likes" your post; she is your friend because she knows you. She jumps on airplanes to host a shower, attend a wedding, quarantine with her husband, and visit her parents. She calls to check in, connects people to others, and points them towards Jesus. Just take a walk with her and her dog, Andy, and you will quickly realize how much she loves people.

Seeds Sown is written for you. Ann will bring you into her journey of cancer, when she walked in the valleys, took the hands of people around her, and most importantly sat at the feet of Jesus and took His strength each day. Ann provides practical, daily steps that you can take to restore your daily habits of nutrition, exercise, and sleep beginning today. Ann is intentional and a conqueror—she is one of my heroes.

I want to encourage you to pull out your highlighters and take notes as you read this book. It is Ann's prayer to watch as *Seeds Sown* bears fruit through you.

SUSIE KOLTERMAN
Ann's FAVORITE sister

INTRODUCTION

Seeds are sown every day. Some seeds are sown in large fields that will be ripe at harvest time with a large crop. Some seeds are sown surrounding homes in gardens that will grow and blossom into beautiful flowers which can be cut and placed in a vase on your table. Some seeds are sown in a vegetable garden which will grow and be harvested as the summer progresses, to be eaten fresh or canned, or frozen to be enjoyed in the winter months.

The seeds that I want to sow with this book are seeds of faith, seeds of intention, and seeds of restoration. These are seeds for your health, all areas of your health—including mind, body, and soul. We work with our doctors primarily to focus on our health concerns with what we eat and how much we move. And those are two essential components that do have a positive impact on our health journey. But when we focus on those two and leave out the other facets of our whole body, we never receive the complete healing that was intended from our Creator.

This book has been building inside of me for years. From various vantage points, I have watched things change in our country's health. As a daughter of a farmer, a nurse, a wife, a mother, and an independent consultant in a health/wellness business, I observed things going well; but I watched many more things going in the wrong direction. And the people who should have been helping "right the ship" were not doing anything. They were silent because they were not bold enough to help people face the hard truths concerning the trajectory of their health. These people didn't have the time, they didn't choose to be change agents, and they didn't know to whom to refer them.

We have had technological and pharmaceutical advances in health care, and our patients have benefitted from them. I also feel, with these advances, we have neglected to focus on the basics. The "shiny" advances capture us, and we have been all about following them. We ignore and don't educate on the simple things that work and significantly impact our health journey.

After many years of observing, learning, and knowing that it all comes back to the foundation of our health, I started writing this book. The seeds I have gleaned that help people's whole lives thrive for the most part are what is being shared in this book. We cannot control everything in our lives, but we are responsible for learning from others and implementing the truths they convey. These seeds of knowledge that we "plant" and "cultivate" through our application and implementation will give our bodies the best chance to not let disease in and take a foothold or hopefully minimize its growth. I experienced a very unexpected diagnosis and decided I needed to share my knowledge to help us all refocus on the basics through faith, intention, and restoration. These encompass our whole bodies, and when we incorporate steps to help each area of our body, our total health benefits.

Thank you for joining me, and may the seeds I share with you add to the total growth of your health.

SEEDS SOWN

CHAPTER 1

A FAITH LIKE PETER'S— STUMBLING IS PART OF THE JOURNEY

"Peter replied, 'Even if all fall away on account of you, I never will.' 'I tell you the truth,' Jesus answered, 'this very night, before the rooster crows, you will disown me three times."

MATTHEW 26:33-34 NIV

March 9, 2021—I was sitting alone in my surgeon's office. I was scared.

I wasn't just physically alone that day. I was mentally alone, too. On Jan 31, 2020, I put my husband on a plane to work in Vermont to start a remote job for what would be the next 2-3 years. We live in Florida, so it wasn't a close commute. Remember what happened in March of 2020? By the Spring of 2021, we were used to the distance. We were having fun exploring the New England states when I visited. But that day in March, as I sat awaiting my surgeon's arrival, I was alone in so many ways. I didn't bring anyone with me. My husband had asked if he should fly down for the appointment; but being the stubborn nurse, I declined his offer. I had reasoned that it was a 20-minute appointment to set up my surgery. It wasn't like the surgeon and I were going to negotiate a sweet deal, and I may get my way and not have to have surgery. I had to have surgery. No questions asked. Why waste a flight for a 20-minute appointment was one of my many thoughts. We agreed that he would be home for the time around my surgery, which would be more critical.

I was still not accepting the news I had been given a few weeks earlier after my colonoscopy. I was 49 and healthy until that fateful day I had blood in my stool in the summer of 2020. It kept occurring. I knew I needed to be evaluated by a physician for the problems I was seeing. In the next few months, because we were new to the area and I wasn't working in the hospital, I asked someone I had met at a yoga class for a referral. She had worked as a nurse manager at a hospital near me, so I knew she would be able to give a credible referral. Also, if you have symptoms, I encourage you not to delay treatment like I did—I should have called right away. Again, I am a nurse; we don't always make the best patients.

The morning of my colonoscopy, I rolled into the outpatient center confident I wanted to be awake for the procedure. I had an unreasonable fear of being put to sleep. I worked in Labor and Delivery (hereafter L/D) and have worked in the OR to help with cesarean sections. I never liked watching as women were put to sleep and liked it less when they woke up from anesthesia. I tried to negotiate with my anesthesiologist, but she looked at me with a smile and said, "Can you just play by the rules and go to sleep like everyone else?" I agreed because she quickly and thoughtfully looked at me and said, "If there is a problem, I will wake you up as the procedure is coming to an end so you can visualize it on the screen." I agreed. She held my hand as she put me to sleep, and I had the best nap ever. That was until she woke me up quietly and said, "Ann, look at the screen." My doctor kindly showed me a large polyp, most likely a tumor she shared quietly. As I woke up more, she shared that this was probably an aggressive form of cancer. My medical team would find out more when the pathologist read the biopsy results. My GI doctor wrote on my discharge instructions the description of the polyp and three surgeons' names to start to research. I would need a portion of my colon removed. I was a bit overwhelmed. And again, I didn't know the surgeons here. I was devastated not to be "in the know" in the medical community. My world was quickly starting to spin out of control.

As the following days passed, I called my new friends here in the area asking for more information on the surgeons' names or any other surgeons that people would share with me. I Googled the options given to me. I called one who came highly recommended to me by a close Bible study friend and I was booked for an appointment a month out. Shoot, even I knew that was not good. I asked to be placed on the cancellation list but knew I needed to be evaluated ASAP by a surgeon.

I called the top surgeon on my list from my GI doctor, and he had an opening the following week. I took it. I hung up the phone and asked myself, "Hold it! Why does he have an opening so quickly? Is he not good?!" Now I was worried. His reviews were pretty good on Google, and the websites that graded him were also good. Yes, I started with Google to research this surgeon. I stewed a little longer. And a day or so later, I remembered our neighbor across the street was a retired anesthesiologist at the hospital where this surgeon works. He was not just one of the anesthesiologists but the Chief of Anesthesiology there until he retired. He knew his stuff and was well respected. He would have to know this potential surgeon and know him well! So, I texted Conway to get the scoop and ran across the street to ask ALL the questions. It took one. Do you know Dr. E? Conway looked at me with a smile, put his thumb up, and said, "He is meticulous." I was relieved. Coworkers are brutally honest about each other; this was a GLOWING recommendation. He gave me a long hug. Ok. Dr. E passed that test. I thanked Conway profusely and walked back across the street. I calmed down for about 5 minutes.

My phone rang the morning of my appointment. The assistant in my surgeon's office told me Dr. E was called away to care for an emergent patient and wanted to know if we could reschedule. "Sure," I quietly said. I wasn't surprised. I know surgeons' schedules and how emergency surgeries come up. I was upset but quickly realized it could be me going for emergency surgery, so I should calm down and be thankful. I quickly bowed my head and prayed for Dr. E and his patient. His surgical skills were needed by someone else emergently. I will meet him next week.

The Day I Met My Surgeon

The following week came; and as I said at the opening, I was sitting alone, scared, in his office. I had an irrational fear of having surgery. Again, nurses don't generally make the best patients, but I hadn't planned to act that way as the situation unfolded. I was still in denial that I needed surgery and the course that followed. I was praying for my polyp to miraculously fall out. I was willing to do almost anything not to experience surgery. I finally, viscerally, understood, after 25+ years as a nurse, why some patients were truly anxious about having a cesarean section. As a nurse, I was so comfortable being in the OR that I had forgotten to put myself in their spot—scared, unfamiliar with hospital procedures, and having someone cut into their body. I was so comfortable being in surgery as a nurse that I forgot it is not something patients do every day. I felt all the feelings entirely and was overwhelmed by them. I was so surprised by my uncertainty as I faced this surgery; it was very much not my usual confident nurse self.

As I sat in the office, God reminded me how He had prepared the path for this time in my life. He not only moved us to Florida but also into the house across the street from Conway. Not to mention the other wonderful neighbors that we called family. More to come on that as I write. I was reminded of a conversation with a Bible study friend a few weeks prior. She had sent a prayer request as she was having unexpected surgery. I prayed for her surgery and that God would guide her surgeon's hands. And then, it dawned on me as we celebrated her positive outcome that she also had surgery at the same hospital in which I was to have mine. I quietly asked who her surgeon was, and she said his name. It was Dr. E. It turns out I had been praying for him as I was contemplating which surgeon to choose. God knew. God is in the details and has our paths laid out for us. All of these details should have kept me calm; but alas, my sight was distracted by the evil one, and you will see more as this unfolds.

The door opened to the office room. My surgeon walked in and calmly said "So, it looks as if you need to have surgery." I quietly agreed. I sheepishly looked up and said, "I am Conway's neighbor. He said that you would take good care of me." He smiled. He remembered him. He then explained what he had reviewed in my recent medical history. He took out a plain sheet of paper, drew a colon, and added where my polyp was. Then he draws two lines where he would take out the section of my colon and reattach it. He made this surgery look so simple. He assured me he should be able to perform it laparoscopically and that my recovery would go smoothly. Simple. At least it was to him. I understood it all medically. It was my mind that was creating a war all around this.

My mind was going fifty thousand directions, and none were good. I know how surgery goes, but I just didn't ever want to be a patient in the OR. Especially a sleeping one. I have control issues. And being asleep in a cold room, having a chunk of my colon removed, and not being familiar with this surgery was a tad disconcerting. The worst part was that my modesty was figuratively being "thrown out the window" during my time in the OR. I have prepped many patients for surgery and knew it was all exposed. Don't ask me why this bothered me, but it did. I knew the drill: You drop your modesty on admission and pick it up on the day of discharge from the hospital. So not comforting as I sat there. It felt like an out-of-body experience.

And then I threw a temper tantrum. I looked at my surgeon and listed off the reasons why I shouldn't be there. I reviewed the most likely causes of colon cancer—I have never smoked, rarely drink alcohol, have never done drugs, am a healthy weight, and eat more veggies than most Americans. I also walk a lot of steps each day with my dog! I don't fit into the "normal" reasons to be diagnosed with cancer. I knew he knew this information better than I did, and listing it off to him was ridiculous. But there I was, saying it anyway.

He looked at me and calmly said, "Disease doesn't follow the rules."

And I quickly became quiet. My surgeon was right. Even though we do a lot of things right, we still experience the effects of a disease, which I know is the direct result of sin. He didn't launch into the faith reference, but that is exactly where my mind went. I realized then that I had a hefty dose of PRIDE and PRIVILEGE that was being stripped away from me with those five words. And those words have echoed in my mind all day long, every day, since. I am unable to stop them from repeating in my mind. I knew as these words kept repeating in my thoughts that God was tugging at me for some reason. But why? This question would be answered later in my journey and ultimately as I write this book.

As I sat with his scheduler to put my surgery on his calendar, I whispered to him, "Will you please not drink the night before my surgery?" I was a mess! Who asks their surgeon not to drink the night before their surgery?! I guess I had just done that. I have prayed multiple times that he didn't hear me say that.

This office visit was episode number 1 of 3 with my surgeon. For someone who regularly tries to be the hands and feet of Jesus and share the Gospel as I meet others, this was a "swing and a miss!" I prayed he would still do an excellent job on my surgery even though I had presented myself so poorly. I walked out to my car and repented for my temper tantrum. I prayed God would forgive me. I knew how to be respectful to doctors, and that day I failed miserably!! It turns out my specific prayers each day going forward had my surgeon on the top of my list. Dear God, please guide his hands during my surgery. And may his memory of this office visit be erased. Amen.

The Day of Surgery

Let me set the stage. I had been awake the whole night before, not all from anxiety. You "get to" do an in-depth lemon-flavored colon prep the day before a colon resection. Not only do you get to do that, you "get to" take some high-dose antibiotics as your colon is the dirtiest place in your body; and minimizing an infection is prudent for this surgery. If you know anything about taking regular antibiotics on an empty stomach, just imagine high-dose antibiotics. I wanted to puke. ALL. NIGHT. LONG. I couldn't close my eyes, or the feeling of nausea was even worse. I was counting the hours until I could be admitted and be able to ask for some Zofran to alleviate the nausea I was experiencing. I was also wondering why I hadn't asked to start my own IV, give myself the antibiotics via IV, and then my stomach and I could have been on much better terms; but he would have thought I was a total nut job. Just when you think it couldn't get any worse, it does. He ordered some electrolyte concoction for me to drink on my way to the hospital. It was watermelon flavored. I HATE watermelon, and there was no chance I was putting anything in my stomach the way I felt that morning. So, that went in the trash as I left for the hospital that morning. The nurse as a patient was not going so well.

I arrived at the hospital in a quiet mood. I couldn't believe today I was having surgery. I hadn't slept. I wanted to throw up. It felt as if I was walking in a daze. I was relieved when I heard the nurse call my name to go back. Her name was Maribel; she was a gift from God. She was kind. She took great care as she did all the routine things I knew would happen. I was thankful my surgeon had not put a sign on my chart that stated I was the "crazy chick." It would have been warranted given our first interaction, though. The anesthesia team came in. I shared that I was Conway's neighbor, and they smiled. They all knew Conway. I was on the good side of my anesthesia team. Whew! I wanted to not only go to sleep, but I wanted to wake up! My surgeon stopped in. He ensured I was ready and asked if I had any other questions. I kept my conversation short and polite. I didn't want another lousy interaction with him before he performed my surgery. Maribel finished everything, hugged me, and, I believe, said a quick prayer with me before I was moved back to the OR on a gurney. Thankfully, the only memory of the OR room was sliding myself over to the OR table. They put me right to sleep. I think my surgeon had told them I could be a handful! I was also thankful that I was asleep during the surgery. Who knows what I would have said if I had spinal anesthesia and had been awake!

The Day After Surgery

But the day after surgery was another thing. My surgeon made rounds early in the morning. Or it seemed early since sleeping the night after surgery is questionable at best. My roommate was up a lot; and our room was right by a substation for the nurses, so dark and quiet didn't happen. I was sitting up and dressed because my night nurse had helped me get out of the ugly hospital gown and into my yoga gear sometime in the middle of the night. My surgeon came in and politely asked how I was doing and then reviewed that the surgery went well. He shared that he removed 8 or 9 inches of my colon, and I shot him the dirtiest look I had. I was pissed that I had lost a chunk of my colon. I still could not accept it was gone.

I knew that much of my colon needed to be removed, and his surgical skills were excellent. But my mind could not and would still not accept it. He looked back at me and said, "You wanted clean edges didn't you?" And I sheepishly replied, "Yes." And we quietly finished our conversation and reviewed what I needed to do on Post Op day one. He left my room. If my dad had been there, I would have been scolded, just like when I was a toddler. You know, when you were a toddler and your dad threatened to take you out of church because you were loud. Yep! That's what I was envisioning. Yikes!

That was episode number 2 of 3 with my surgeon. I once again was mortified by my behavior. I couldn't walk to my car, so I had to sit in my hospital bed and ask for forgiveness. What was I doing? Why was I acting like this? Patients are generally thankful as they talk to their surgeons the day after surgery. I have witnessed it countless times as a nurse. Why was I allowing my doubt to be greater than my faith?? This pattern was not good.

Recovery went well. When I saw my surgeon the following two days, I behaved better. I didn't say much. I did everything I should do to get out of the hospital in a timely fashion. I was discharged by my surgeon from the hospital on post-op day 3.

He called me the next week to tell me the results of my pathology report and that my polyp was, in fact, cancer. Three lymph nodes were involved, and I needed to undergo chemotherapy to treat the cancerous growth. I would follow up with him in two weeks. He would help me make a plan and give me referrals. The two-week check-up went well, and I found out that he would place my port soon after and referred me to a highly qualified oncologist. The port placement also was uneventful. He actually managed to crack a surgeon joke with me in pre-op, so I knew he didn't hate me and hadn't lost all hope in me either.

Two Weeks Later

I was alone psychologically in the same room at my surgeon's office. Unbeknownst to my surgeon, our lives had been, metaphorically speaking, turned upside down with more unexpected changes. My husband's career had fallen apart since my surgeon placed my port two weeks ago.

As I approached the office, I promised myself I would not say more than I needed to at this appointment. I was a mess emotionally, and I just wanted my surgeon to assess my surgical site so I could get out. I wanted to return home where I felt safe and could process everything in silence. When things are falling apart in my life, I tend to clam up before I process it with my peeps.

But then he came in and asked how I was doing. I looked at him and quietly said, "That is a loaded question…Surgically, I am ok. Can you just examine me so I can go home?" I wanted to leave quickly. But he heard the uneasiness in my voice. I don't think he was ready for what would be shared next.

I unloaded it all. I shared everything that happened to us, and it went something like this.

"As I headed into my first day of chemotherapy three days after you had placed my port, I was not only scared about the whole chemotherapy thing. But I knew my husband and 500 other workers would likely lose their jobs that day. The company he had moved to Vermont over a year earlier to help turn around, didn't. They folded. Not only quickly but badly. I had texted my husband, 'Please don't call me while I am getting my first dose of chemo and tell me you lost your job. I will call you after.' And I did. And they had closed the company that day during my chemotherapy administration. We had no cobra for health insurance. The company did not provide any severance pay. The company was completely out of money. Goodbye, and good luck were essentially the sentiments they said to all employees. My husband and others had just completely lost their income. Thankfully I worked enough hours at my job to transfer our health insurance coverage to them, but that meant delaying my next round of chemo until the new insurance company had approved it."

I was like a fire hose on HIGH! I had just "vomited" every detail of our lives to him. How embarrassing. That post-op visit turned into a Psych visit in a hot minute. I wanted to crawl into a hole. And quickly.

My surgeon was stunned and shared his apologies. And as he opened the exam room door for me, he firmly said, "You go this way." And he pointed me to the exit of his office.

That was episode number 3 of 3. I didn't anticipate unloading all my problems on my surgeon. I was mortified with my behavior, yet again. I walked to my car. I repented to God again and thought, God help me! What is going on? I know I can entirely depend on Jesus! And here I am, just like Peter that late Thursday night of Jesus' crucifixion. My actions looked like I had zero faith in You! I was unstable. I was distracted by all of the problems occurring in our lives. I had denied Your existence entirely with all the anxiety I let loose in front of my surgeon. God, you have been faithful each step of the way. And all I could do was focus on the crap Satan was slinging at us!

I didn't realize it then, but I fully understand how Peter felt the night he walked toward Jesus on the water. When his eyes were on Jesus, he could walk ON THE WATER, but when he looked at the waves, he would sink. For whatever reason, when I was with my surgeon, I saw the waves; I took my eyes off Jesus and started to drown. I gulped in the water of fear. All of the unknowns of my diagnosis crushed me, and I took it all out on him. He unknowingly walked in on the worst chapter of my life so far and cared for me despite my less-than-appealing way of dealing with this life-changing diagnosis.

One Year After My Surgery

Fast forward about a year, and my husband needed hernia surgery; guess whose office we were sitting back in a year to the date of my surgery. I was sitting in the corner trying to blend into the wallpaper on the wall when he came in. He greeted my husband, looked at me, and said slowly, with a voice that dropped with each word, "I remember...you." I didn't leave a good memory in his mind, and I didn't blame him. He had seen the worst of me. Thankfully, my husband's surgery went well, and all I had to do was answer the call from Dr. E and say thank you for taking care of my husband. I managed not to mess up that conversation.

Authenticity

It's hard to share the worst part at first, but I wanted to paint an accurate picture of myself and the reality of each of us. None of us have picture-perfect lives. We have some pretty ugly days in this earthly life. I believe in Jesus, but know I am a sinner. I repent and ask for forgiveness; and then sometimes, I go back and make the same mistake or commit the same sin again. As you read, I want you to understand that I don't think I am all that and a bag of chips. Or guess I have a higher understanding of faith and my walk is pretty impressive, as you have read. My walk veers off that path just like yours has. That's a "perk" of sinful living. We all fall. But, if we believe in him, we have a Savior in Jesus that has forgiven our sins on that cross about 2000 years ago. The good news of the Gospel means we can get back up and get back on God's path for our lives.

I crumbled many times after discovering I had colon cancer and knowing the steps I would have to walk as my body was restored to health. I wasn't unique in my diagnosis. But I now know God had an individual purpose for me with my diagnosis. He was going to take my awful mess and turn it into a message that would proclaim His glory. God has always been present in my life and continues to be present today. I doubted the process in my journey, but He remains faithful every day of our lives. He is El Shaddai, God Almighty.

Our faith is shared in many ways throughout our lives. Most people think of it in formal methods. They picture a church, a pastor preaching a sermon, and some old hymns sung by the choir. Other people imagine women sitting over a steaming cup of coffee at their local coffee house, with one woman sharing her story of how she was introduced to faith in Christ. Her friend, who isn't a believer, can hear the complete story, which includes a dramatic climax and a picture-perfect setting. Those dramatic faith stories are rare. Most stories of faith development are simple. Most accounts have many chapters before their hearts were opened to Jesus by the Holy Spirit. Some faith stories come to fruition just before the person is about to die after a life of hard choices. Most people who learn about Jesus learn because a friend, coworker, or random acquaintance becomes their friend; and as their relationship deepens, the conversations just happen. There isn't a "plan to share Jesus" in three quick steps.

Most of the time, the best way to share our faith is to communicate when we stumbled and fell the hardest. Many people can relate to us when we are vulnerable because they have fallen too. Most people share only the highlights of their lives and their success stories. When we dare to share the worst parts of our lives and how God resurrected our mess through His perfect plan, that's when people listen and connect with us. I know your life has not been an easy journey. I know you have experienced bad times and days you wished you could have a do-over. Because of Jesus, we can each have a do-over. Some of us have the privilege of having many do-overs. He has compassion and offers forgiveness through his death and resurrection.

Your response may be, "I don't want to share my mistakes. Someone will make fun of me or think less of me." Most will echo this phrase, "If someone thinks less of you for being honest and authentic, they are not whom you want to be associated with." I encourage you to share the ugly parts of your life with close family or friends when you feel comfortable. Faith matures when the "weeds" of sin attempt to take over our lives, but then we see how God steps in and pulls those weeds. We see our lives become a harvest of his faithfulness, forgiveness, and love that we can share and give Him the glory.

As you know Him, the unexpected diagnosis may not rock you as hard as you think. When you fall off the path, getting back up and attaining your goals will not seem as dire. And as you walk closer with Jesus each day, you will understand that your ultimate goal is to have eternal life with Him.

We will continue, and you will see how faith becomes an integral part of our bodies' restoration process. This perspective may be a new way to look at your health journey. You may not have thought that faith plays a part in your health. It does. I am not saying that you need to spread your faith to have guaranteed health. My prayer is that sharing your faith in Jesus will help your journey in all its ways.

Questions to Journal

What has held you back from sharing your most challenging stories?

How has someone authentically sharing with you about their life experiences helped give you a better perspective on a specific area of your current journey?

Have you walked in on someone else's lowest point and mischaracterized them?

_____

_____

_____

_____

_____

_____

_____

_____

_____

_____

_____

_____

_____

CHAPTER 2

A FAITH LIKE ABRAHAM'S— FAITH PASSED FROM GENERATION TO GENERATION

"We will not hide them from their descendants; we will tell the next generation the praiseworthy deeds of the Lord, his power, and the wonders he has done. He decreed statutes for Jacob and established the law in Israel, which he commanded our ancestors to teach their children, so the next generation would know them, even the children yet to be born, and they in turn would tell their children. Then they would put their trust in God and would not forget his deeds but would keep his commands."

PSALM 78:4-7 NIV

When you are first diagnosed with any disease, you can have a wide range of emotions and reactions. I had reached a point in my journey where I needed to get hold of myself and stay focused. I couldn't let myself swing so wide with my emotions. Someone once said, "You can curl up in your closet in the fetal position for 24 hours; but after that, you need to stand up, put on your big girl panties and deal with it!"

There is a lot of truth with a good dose of humor intertwined in that quote. And after many calls with my sister, it finally came to me to ask God to minimize the swing in my emotional pendulum. As I have described, my emotions were running wild; and I would not be able to help God out as He healed me if I ran around like a chicken with its head cut off. My sister and I immediately started praying for my emotions to stabilize, and God answered those prayers and continues to answer them daily. I laid all of my emotions out—anxiety, fear, confidence, complete belief, and everything in between. I opened my Bible and a notebook, and started writing out Scripture that I could read quietly or aloud. These verses all are encouraging and reassure how God is in control. Over time, as I said these verses, I could feel my emotions start to stabilize. When I felt my emotions sliding to the anxious side, I would quickly recite one of the Scriptures to bring my focus back to God's sovereignty. Satan is constantly trying to get us to question God; reference Genesis 3. When we stay focused on God, Satan is generally kept "at bay." God is stronger than anything Satan can throw at us. Those Scriptures and then my "playlist" were my go-to options to "put on my armor of God" each morning. I remembered that I needed to tell my mountains about my God, and not tell God about my mountains. I was thankful for my faith that was planted by all of my relatives, and I knew I needed to dig deeper into my faith during this journey.

My surgeon laid out my plan of care and it was confirmed by my oncologist. There is a recipe for treating and conquering colon cancer. There are some variables for the "recipe." My diagnosis was based on a tumor removed by surgery, three lymph nodes involved, and no metastasis. We had a very informative first appointment with my oncologist. He and his Nurse Practitioner were educated well and explained all the medications and side effects. They made no promises but were encouraging and shared how the surveillance goes during and after chemotherapy.

Ann's Chemo Recipe

- 12 administrations of 5FU chemotherapy given every two weeks
- Chemotherapy is infused mainly on Mondays and switched to a pump I would take home and continue to infuse at a much lower rate for the next 48 hours.

I was introduced to the chemo team afterward, and they shared more information. It was a little overwhelming, but I kept listening and asking questions as they arose. I had a 24-hour number to call with any questions. I knew I was never alone. WIN. I was not a massive fan of chemo; I knew it was essentially a poison being injected into me, but it also had a ton of research around it's use. Medical decisions are personal, and you will have opinions from both sides. That's a part of every decision you make in life. There is a huge difference between knowing when to listen, when to disregard people's opinions, and when to listen and take note of the facts people share with you.

This recommendation will be one of my first of many encouragements to "find your tribe." No matter what your diagnosis may be or your goal, others are out there that can shed light for you on your journey ahead, including the what ifs. Most people are happy to share their knowledge, will be in your corner, and will give you a convenient way to connect with them. It may not be someone you know, but sometimes a friend of yours will introduce you to someone who will be your mentor for a chapter of your journey. Your tribe can make these rough spots a bit smoother.

At this point, I had not shared my information on social media, but I had a group through my business that I decided to share with on a closed social media group to add a few more prayer partners. And to my surprise, one of the gals reached out to me via a private message that blew my socks off! She had experienced a very similar journey with colon cancer and had just celebrated her one year of being cancer free. She is also in the medical field and is wicked smart, so we reconnected. She quickly became a strong prayer warrior. She gave me a detailed playbook of her journey. She gave me HOPE. Miss Toni was my "wingman" throughout my journey, and still is to this day. We had similar but different journeys. But to have someone who just walked this journey and was willing to walk alongside me was priceless. She shared her emotions with me and encouraged me ahead of any low points. She inspired me in every interaction we had. She was a glowing example of what I wanted to do after conquering this cancer with God's help.

I immediately felt God opening the door to be a voice in an area I hadn't before thought I would have one—educating and encouraging others to live healthier in ALL areas of their lives based on their faith.

Let me take the time to share my faith story with you. I want to shed light on how my faith foundation was formed. Throughout this book, you will see how my faith has grown, and how it has impacted my whole life. You will notice that our reactions to different events in our lives will show how having a strong faith doesn't mean you will not wander or feel overwhelmed. Lean in and have a first-hand look at my journey.

The Unfolding of My Faith

My faith story starts before me and is entirely not about me. It is about how Jesus called me to him. He formed each of us before the creation of this world. God numbered the hairs on our heads and the days of our lives; and the plans for our lives had already been laid out for each of us. He has known who was a chosen child of His from the beginning. God knew when we would come to our saving faith through Him in our lives. He knows our stories intimately, and I am privileged to share mine through His promptings.

As I stated, my faith story started before I was born. Faithful generations before me prayed for each generation that followed. And those prayers continue to be answered with the birth of each child in our family. They prayed we would know Jesus and come to have a deep personal relationship with Him. They didn't just tell us. They lived obediently to Christ and served Christ in everything they did. They attended a church planted in a small "town" around 1880, named Hanover. They also built a school by the church to provide a Christian education for their children. They worked as an extended family to integrate their faith into their farming by praying daily and knowing God would be faithful with each harvest, with the growth of their herds, and with the time spent helping each other with the different steps of farming. My Grandma Glienke taught each of her grandchildren and great-grandchildren this phrase,

---

"Plant with hope, harvest with thanksgiving."

It comes from the Bible verse, Galatians 6:9—"Let us not become weary in doing good for at the proper time we will reap a harvest if we do not give up." The conversations in our family and this community were, and still are to this day, to start with God and end each day with praise for His faithfulness.

Because past generations were all members of the same church, they had different responsibilities through the years to help the church grow in membership through discipling all ages and inviting neighbors to attend with them. Their faithfulness has served them well through the good and lean years. And today, our church in Hanover is still my favorite church to attend. It's not about who the Pastor is or who is playing the organ that Sunday. It's Whom we are worshiping. Many of my family members have passed on and are in heaven, but it still feels as if they are in the pews with us. It's pretty hard to describe, but the experience is felt; and it is like no other.

And being born into this family, my siblings, many of my cousins, close friends and I were baptized into God's family shortly after we were born. I was baptized nine days after I was born. My parents, grandparents, aunts/uncles, and many of my friend's parents were crucial to my upbringing in Christ. This "village" took their part seriously in raising their families to know Jesus. From the sun's rising to the sun's setting, Jesus led their lives. And with everything they did, they built our faith. Each of us, through conversation, church attendance, time in the fields, etc., built our faith. The "village" all played a part...and as I have grown up, I have realized that we all play a role in everyone's faith journey. Our actions, our language, the relationships we cultivate, our character, our work ethic, etc., impacts everyone. We are like a pebble dropped into a still lake. Our Christian life can be a blessing to others if we obediently serve our living Savior, Jesus Christ.

Two additional moments played an integral part in my faith. The first was the day I was confirmed in the Spring of my 8th grade. After 8 years of weekly study and education, we affirmed our faith over two Sundays. The first Sunday we answered questions about all parts of our faith. Our Pastor asked and we answered those questions in front of our congregation. The following Sunday we were confirmed. We were able to choose a verse that meant a lot to us. I picked Psalm 23:1-2 NIV "The Lord is my shepherd, I shall not be in want. He makes me lie down in green pastures, he leads me beside quiet waters." This verse has comforted me and reminded me that Jesus is EVER PRESENT in my life. Every second of my life, Jesus is with me.

The additional moment was on the day I married my husband. My dad's brother was a minister, and he agreed to perform our wedding service. In the midst of all the nervousness, when my Uncle Hermie started his message for us, God stilled my mind; and I listened to each word. His message centered on the verse from Joshua 24:15 NIV "But as for me and my household, we will serve the Lord." Hermie passed on the message that he, my father, and all of their siblings had grown up with—that God is the head of our home. He was passing on the message my Grandma had taught all of us to order our lives, Faith, Family, Farming. And the last but most important underlying message he passed on was this: When we serve the Lord and teach our children to serve the Lord, we will have given the next generations the opportunity to NOT miss out on the gift of heaven. We have been married for over 30 years. And that verse hangs on a plaque on the wall, and in some homes I have stenciled it on our kitchen wall. Our kids know the verse and understand the importance of it as well as we do. From generation to generation, God is good.

Faith in Jesus is simple and complex. While the complex parts are important, I want you to understand the simple parts. First, Jesus loves you and is always with you. Second, love Jesus. Third, read His story in the Bible, worship Him during church services, and build your relationship with Jesus as you talk with others, asking questions as you grow your faith. Keep it simple, but know it is a lifelong journey and not a straight trajectory. Embrace it. It will change your eternal life.

Let's continue and take the next step that will encourage us to deepen our relationship with God, repent of our sins and ask for forgiveness, and learn what a mighty God we serve! It is a step-by-step process, but we can learn and grow together as we open up to the transformation God will accomplish in our progress.

Questions to Journal

Do you know Jesus? This question can be whether you know of Him or that you truly know Jesus.

What is your faith story? For those of you who do not know Jesus, you have a faith story too. The story BEFORE you encounter Jesus is TOTALLY part of your story.

What is your 30-second faith story?

What is your extended 3-5 minute faith story if someone asks for more details?

_____

_____

_____

_____

_____

_____

_____

_____

_____

_____

_____

CHAPTER 3

A FAITH LIKE MOSES'—EQUIPPED BY LIFE EXPERIENCES

> "But Moses said to God, "Who am I, that I should go to
> Pharaoh and bring the Israelites out of Egypt?"
>
> EXODUS 3:11 NIV
>
> "I will help you speak and teach you what to say."
>
> Exodus 4:12 NIV

When you receive a significant diagnosis, you need to share the news. How much do I want to share and to whom do I want to share it with? I am a nurse raised under HIPAA law. I wanted to protect my health privacy as not everyone needed to know all the details. My closest people needed to know as they would pray for me. Please, God, help me discern how to reach out to those in my "need-to-know" circle.

God's Equipping Begins Before This Chapter of My Life

We were in the midst of COVID, and people were sharing more things about their medical life publicly than I had ever seen before. I didn't want to be "that." As I have shared, I was blown away that I had a cancer diagnosis after living a healthier lifestyle over the last 15+ years. I didn't fit the mold and felt "embarrassed" that this dreaded disease had snuck into my body and had a foothold. I didn't want to seek public attention because of my diagnosis. I didn't want anyone to "look" at me and feel sorry. I had to figure out how and why I wanted to share the information, especially if it was going to be public at some point. I needed some people to know. I needed a prayer team immediately.

I started by calling a few. Then the group grew to much larger than a few. And I knew I had more than a few people who were on my side and would shepherd me, pray for me, and want to know how I was doing. I was not ready to put it out on social media, but I needed a way to communicate quickly with a large group. Then I remembered the website www.caringbridge.org; I could pick whom I wanted to invite, and only they would be notified of my updates—done and dusted. I set up a site and shared my updates on that platform.

Since that pre-op appointment with Dr. E, I heard him telling me, "Disease doesn't follow the rules," 24/7 in my brain. Along with that, it felt as if I should be doing something with what I have learned through my journey with health/wellness and my knowledge as a nurse. I knew I could share with people what I had learned. I knew when I was comfortable, I wasn't going to mind telling my story to a broader group. And through all this learning, I connected dots I had not previously thought about as I looked at them singularly. There were so many holes in our health care, and I discovered them because of what was happening to me. I didn't want anyone else to feel as though they were missing valuable parts of their care plan when they needed it the most.

I have shared that I became a student of all the details of my journey and took notes from the beginning. These notes were filling up a notebook. I also worked with a naturopathic doctor who educated me weekly. More notes. And all those people with oncology backgrounds shared their pearls of wisdom. More notes kept being added to my notebook. I realized that I had something special coming together. I just needed to be patient and let God time this out and organize it.

And then God did. It's always God. It's always His timing.

One hundred sixty-two days after my diagnosis, God prompted me to go "Live" on Facebook and share my story. He equipped me with the words, why, and how to make it not about me. And so, I opened up my phone, turned on FB live, and shared authentically. I shared my diagnosis, my surgery, and where I was in my chemotherapy treatment. It was the start of my journey to be an educator and an advocate, not only on colon cancer detection but encompassing the whole story of our health. The story includes our faith walk, food choices, the importance of activity, shattering some comfort zones, backing things up with solid research, and being authentic. And that's what I continue to do on social media and many interactions. I educate, share recipes, share credible research on health and colon cancer, and share my progress. I have shared the good and the ugly parts of my journey because cancer and chemotherapy are not a joy ride.

So many good things have come from sharing my story. The private messages which say, "I had my colonoscopy, and I am ALL CLEAR!" The texts saying thank you for helping them to be brave to make the call; that they are being seen for this symptom or this development. Many questions about how to change their eating habits have been asked and answered. The questions from others with a new diagnosis also want to know how I learned what I did.

When I obeyed God and started sharing, I wanted to help at least one person. I thought it was worth it if one person got an early diagnosis. It is worth it if one person changes their eating or exercise habits and minimizes their risk for any chronic disease. If my authenticity decreases the number of calls any surgeon has to make to a patient to tell them they have cancer, it is worth it. You never forget the sound of your surgeon's voice on the other end of the phone when they give you the news. They talk slowly and lower their tone. It has to be one of the most challenging parts of their job. And if I can do anything to help them make one fewer phone call, I am ALL IN.

The Next Steps of Being Equipped

And then one video call with my sister, her husband in the background listening, they said the words I didn't want to commit to at all. They both simultaneously said, "Ann, you have to write a book." And I was like, ugh! No. Can't I just talk? And they reminded me that people who write books are more likely to be invited to share their stories publicly. I was not opposed to writing a book, but I felt completely unprepared and in no way equipped. I didn't know the first thing about it and was overwhelmed about how to start writing. There are a lot of steps to getting published, and I wasn't even sure how to find a publisher.

And then one Sunday at church, God answered the prayer about a publisher. Our church has a team of Pastors, so each Sunday, you can hear from a different one. And this Sunday was Pastor Goodlet's day to give the sermon. Ironically, he shared his story about his journey as a Pastor at our church. And how each year, he has met with our Senior Pastor to talk about goals and how he felt God was leading him. A few years ago, when he met with our Senior Pastor, he shared that he didn't feel he was supposed to pursue being a teaching Pastor. He had felt led to start a publishing company. I about dropped the pen I was taking notes with as he said those words. God—right timing. Right person. Right story. It turns out I knew of a publisher now. That's one step in the process of writing a book that I needed. Thank you, God.

But what about the others? I wasn't sure exactly how I should write this book. I had a lot of ideas and notes scratched in a notebook. I had some pillars that I thought would be good to focus on in the book. But how do you start? I wasn't ready to commit to a publisher yet, but I knew I had to start organizing each of these ideas.

Equipped Through Exercise

I walk my dog a lot. We generally walk twice a day. During chemo, my pace was abysmal, and my distance walked varied depending on the week of treatment. But I found myself on these walks listening to God. I don't wear earphones. I just walk. And those walks were unlike any walks I have had before. I just became silent in my mind and let God talk to me. I allow Him to generate ideas. I let Him walk me through ways to write this book. I let Him filter stories into my mind to use as examples in my writing.

Sometimes I would have a specific question or part of the book I was trying to figure out how to bring to life through writing. Sometimes the ideas I thought were winners became drafts 3, 6, or even more. I had a few people I bravely shared my first drafts with, and they were kind to me. This book started pretty rough as my ideas were jumbled and awkward. Each walk I took, God gave me ideas that I have implemented. Formal education is not the only way to learn and be equipped for our new journey. I have no education in writing or English, except for the required courses in high school and college.

I read a book a few years ago called The Circle Maker by Mark Batterson. I had never thought about how we should "circle our prayers" around what we wanted to do or achieve. But this idea is precisely what he had described throughout his book. I was walking out my prayers. Every step I took, God was talking to me. Sometimes the conversation was quiet, and that was good, too. The most creative ideas come in those still, quiet moments. This book is the culmination of the inspiration given to me by God over every walk I have taken this last year.

Equipped Through Education

This step is the most obvious to most of you and me. We are bound to learn when we sit down and focus on something. We can learn by taking a class, reading a book, or attending a conference. Some things do require some formal education. You can also find a mentor to learn from over time in the area of growth you seek.

I have a nursing background, and I felt I was a step ahead on the medical information in some aspects. I had been learning a lot about health/wellness because of a business I joined—the people I met, the information they educated us on, and the speakers they brought in. I also became an avid reader of a wide variety of topics. I have a substantial library of books I have read over the years, some of which I have shared in the back of the book under Resources. Please review the suggestions and read the ones that will add value to your journey.

We should not stop learning after we graduate from our respective schools. There is so much available to us because of technology and the availability of goods in our society. And being open to learning beyond our comfort zone is a significant step in our life journey. I will be honest that you need to have a firm foundation and be able to tell the truth from untruth, because many things are being shared untruthfully in this world. Be astute in your learning and don't follow just anyone. It is an essential step to 'vet' whom you are listening to, reading, or the research that you are investigating.

Equipped Through Connections

When problems started to be detected in my health, I had a qualified referral source for my colonoscopy. God provided me with excellent referrals at each step because of whom I had connected with along the way. God has prepared our way. He sets up the people we are to meet along the way and assists us in growing the relationships, and He also equips us with the knowledge that we will need at just the right time. Sometimes, the learning is quicker and in a more urgent manner.

As I was seeking care for my diagnosis and treatment, I would share with my caregivers that I was a nurse, an L/D nurse. I would kindly remind them that I do not know much, if anything, about colon problems and cancer. And then, I would kindly ask if they could explain everything in more detail as I wanted to understand fully how this would affect my body, how I would heal, and how my body would tolerate chemotherapy. My care teams were so kind and always answered my many questions. To further support my learning curve, I connected with a naturopathic doctor, Tanda Cook. I wasn't thrilled to be putting the poison of chemo in my body, but I also knew that someone with her knowledge base could help me immensely. Her care focused on the foods I ate, exercise, sleep, deep breathing, and other details I would never have known to implement. I will explain it in more detail when I focus on nutrition later in the book. I also connected with the nurses I knew who had worked in oncology. I asked them many questions about chemo, side effects, best practices, etc. Each person I reached out to gave me a clearer picture of what I would go through. The more I knew, the better I felt…mostly. I was still pretty apprehensive, but I think this goes along with diagnosis of cancer or any chronic disease.

Like Moses, our faith isn't just grown on Saturday at Temple or Sunday at church. Faith and health are developed and spread by each of the choices we make in our lives. People are watching everyone who makes both unsuccessful and successful choices in their lives. They analyze how those choices were decided upon and how they created the path of success for each person. We must remember that we can each make the "same" decisions and still have different outcomes. We are not carbon copies of each other. God uniquely creates us, and the "same" choices that are made, especially in health, will not guarantee the same outcome for each individual, especially in the discipline of cancer development and treatment.

All parts of our lives overlap. And that's why I thought Moses' life was a great example of sharing how faith has been used to equip us in our life. God works in all the details of our life—He is the God of our faith, our whole being, and our whole life. The Ten Commandments God gave to Moses exemplify how faith interacts throughout our lives. They start with faith and worship, focusing on God, then progress to honoring family and life's sanctity, preserving marriage, not stealing, honesty, and discipline. The Ten Commandments are the foundation of the Jewish and Christian faiths.

Moses had some areas he knew he needed help in and some that God grew him in that he may not want to admit. I believe we can all resonate with that. And I encourage you to look back and see how you focused on some hard-to-grow-in areas and how that matured you. A bit harder place is doing a self-evaluation. Start writing down areas that you know need attention, but hate to admit are a problem. You may not be ready for that step, but it will shift the trajectory of your future to a whole new level when you focus on the most challenging parts, and with the help of God, you fix them. I will dig deeper into this in Chapter 11.

Maybe as you look at the growth you have been working on in your life, you have never equated it with God's guidance or that He has been equipping you. I haven't and don't always either. This experience stopped me in my tracks, and I have done more soul searching and looked more closely for God in the details. I have seen more distinctly how God has orchestrated it all. I can't take credit for any of it. But if reading this book can help any of you see God working more in your life, that would be an answer to one of the many prayers I have prayed as I write this book.

SEEDS SOWN

Questions to Journal

How has God been equipping or growing me?

Which area(s) can I see that need improvement? Which area(s) do I not want to admit need work?

Have I taken time to listen to God for direction and the equipping I need to serve him going forward?

_____

_____

_____

_____

_____

_____

_____

_____

_____

_____

_____

_____

_____

CHAPTER 4

A FAITH LIKE JOSEPH'S— WISDOM ACQUIRED

"for gaining wisdom and instruction; for understanding words of insight; for receiving instruction in prudent behavior, doing what is right and just and fair; for giving prudence to those who are simple, knowledge and discretion to the young—let the wise listen and add to their learning, and let the discerning get guidance—for understanding proverbs and parables, the sayings and riddles of the wise. The fear of the Lord is the beginning of knowledge, but fools despise wisdom and instruction."

PROVERBS 1:2-7 NIV

Wisdom. Knowledge. Well-educated. Intelligent. Brilliant.

These are the words that point to people we seek answers or direction from as we are learning. We want to learn from those with more education and knowledge than we have. We seek input from those with letters behind their name, which they earned through years of higher education. We look for credible research from our universities to make good decisions in all areas of our lives.

Those qualifiers can lead us astray if we focus only on the knowledge, well-educated, intelligent, and brilliant aspects of those from whom we obtain information. We need to focus on those people who possess wisdom, Godly wisdom. Those in our lives who have much intelligence can lack wisdom. And if we seek intelligence without wisdom, it will lead us down a path that leads to destruction. As is noted in Proverbs 1:7 NIV, "The fear of the LORD is the beginning of knowledge, but fools despise wisdom and discipline." Do you notice the important details? When we fear the LORD, we will obtain knowledge; but if we despise wisdom and discipline, we are fools. Take note as this verse is the theme of the book of Proverbs.

I want to share a few ways I have obtained wisdom based on God's Word. In Chapter 2, I shared how my family shared their faith from generation to generation; and by sharing their faith, they imparted wisdom in each step of their lives. Now, I would like to share with you three additional times that gave me opportunities to obtain wisdom.

ROCK (Raising Our Christian Kids) Bible Study

There is always an opportunity at our churches to join a Bible Study. At each church we have belonged to, I have found one or two I have joined. When we moved to a western suburb of Minneapolis, we joined a church; and I soon found myself invited and attending the Bible Study group for moms, led by some other moms. The year I joined, Wendy and Denise were the leaders. We gathered about ten or so other ladies in one of our basement conference rooms in our church. We met weekly and studied different topics in the years we met.

These mornings found us all at different points on our faith and family journeys. We gathered and opened our Bibles and our study books. We learned together and asked each other questions; and as we answered, we dug into our

Bibles to ensure our answers aligned with what God had written. We grew together in all areas of our lives as we studied Jesus' Word. We laughed, we cried, and we prayed. Our studies deepened and spilled over some years into the summer months as we enjoyed our time together and didn't want to have much time apart.

Our family experienced some difficult years when we lived in Minnesota. The church family that God surrounded us with at this time weathered the storms with us. They gathered close when the waves crashed wildly around us and celebrated with each step that God miraculously healed. As our children hit milestones in their faith, we all were present at those services. Our family members still remember the sermon that was shared by Pastor Snow when our oldest son was confirmed. We still talk about how he used a full-size mirror and some cardboard cutouts representing the Ten Commandments. As he closed the sermon, he positioned the cardboard cutouts on the mirror, and what we saw as a congregation was the cross that reflected from the design of the cutouts. He had tied the law of the Ten Commandments to the gift of forgiveness of Christ's death and resurrection in a visual that we still talk about years later.

Our mom's Bible Study times added wisdom to our lives as we studied God's true Word. We learned each time we gathered together as we quieted our minds and opened our hearts to understand. That is one of the ways God imparts His wisdom. It can be as simple as a group of moms gathering weekly with their Bibles in a basement conference room. Nothing fancy and not world-renowned. Growing wisdom and faith in Jesus in the simple moments seems simple, but God works in our everyday moments. We need to be on purpose each minute that we live. God doesn't want us to waste a moment. He also wants us to know that the moments don't have to be extravagant to gain His wisdom. You can invite some friends to sit around your kitchen table. Gather, open up your Bibles, and ask God to bless your time together. It will surely add peace and contentment to all areas of your life. Wisdom does that. It prepares you for each hill and valley you will encounter. When those unexpected things happen, they don't entirely overwhelm but feel more like a speed bump because your foundation is firmly planted in God's wisdom.

BSF (Bible Study Fellowship)

I worked with an excellent and kind nurse named Juli in a Minneapolis area hospital. Juli is the epitome of kind and loving. If you are familiar with the Fruit of the Spirit listed in Galatians, Juli embodies them all. We worked many shifts together and became friends through the years. I wanted to be more like Juli. I had some rough edges that softened as I learned from her through our many conversations. In these conversations, she would share about a Bible study she went to and ask me to go with her. I wanted to go, but it was on the same day and time as ROCK. The best part was she kept asking me for a few years, and I kept saying no. I just couldn't pull myself away from the study at my church. Thank you Juli for your persistence in inviting me to BSF.

My answer changed when she shared that they had opened up another class of her Bible Study that she attended, and it was closer to me and on a different day of the week. I knew I had to say yes. On a Wednesday in March of 2006, I walked into a church hosting this Bible Study with many women and children. There were about 400 women in the sanctuary as I sat by myself that first day. I hadn't attended a Bible study with that many women! What was this? Juli had shared some details, but what I experienced that day was pretty profound. They were studying Genesis. I will never forget the gal who welcomed us and shared that she was filling in for Patti as she was with her husband in Japan for a business trip. Those few details led me to a distinct realization. I knew our hospital's CEO was in Japan for a Six Sigma training. Did I just learn that the CEO of my hospital was a Christian, and his wife was the leader of this Bible Study? I found out both of those things were true.

The new people were excused to a separate small group to learn more about Bible Study Fellowship while the other women went to their small groups. During that time, I learned a lot about this Bible Study group, and I was intrigued and wanted to attend more. If you are curious about Bible Study Fellowship, please visit www.bsfinternational.org to learn more and find a class near you. Before we left the group, we were given a lesson for the following week. I quickly skimmed it and couldn't wait to study.

They excused us to go back into the sanctuary for the lecture. A lecture? What? I had brought only my Bible. I didn't know I needed a notebook to take notes. I sat and listened. I scribbled some things in my Bible as Candace shared about the chapter of Genesis they were studying. I was blown away by how she unpacked the truths and the points that pointed to our Savior, Jesus, in this chapter of Genesis.

They placed us into a small group the next week of attending BSF. In the first class I attended in a Minneapolis area class, I found three women who became my tribe. We sat in the same place each week, as two of us were nurses and on the "medical" team. Melanie, Heather, Nancy, and I became BSF sisters and were never separated those mornings. We weren't always in the same small group, but we were friends for life. Melanie, Heather, and I are still friends across the miles as I have moved away. These women have made me sharper and more robust in pursuing my relationship with Christ through our years in BSF.

BSF has a unique philosophy; and because of that, men and women and their children who attend a BSF class will grow in Godly wisdom. BSF has one resource—the Bible. That is all we study and reference as we learn each week. The notes provided are rooted in the Scripture. The questions posed to us each week are focused on a study in the Bible's passages and other verses that further help us focus on the truth we are studying. Each part is created to emphasize the other—the questions, the small-group time, the lecture, and the notes. These four parts help everyone learn more deeply. This class impacts all generations; and wisdom is taught weekly, year by year across the globe.

A Sentence in a Book That Clarified My Study

I can't remember in which book I read this sentence: "My mentor shared that he had studied Proverbs for ten years in a row. He read a chapter of Proverbs each day of the month and repeated it every month for ten years." I reread that sentence. Again and again. Ten years. Month after month. Really? And then it dawned on me. His mentor, which meant that the person he was working with was many steps ahead of him in multiple areas, had studied Proverbs for ten years. I noted that and decided I would start the next month, January 2019. I have read many good ideas in books throughout the years, but this was a God idea; and it nudged me to take note and act on it. That was the Holy Spirit working in my life to prepare me for this moment. God knew I needed a lot of equipping to bring me to a point where I would be more prepared to write this book.

Step 1: January 2019—I purchased a devotional for Proverbs and used my Bible. Proverbs has 31 chapters, and you read a chapter each day of the month. Day 1, read chapter 1.

Step 2: February—I purchased another devotional to add to my morning routine. Other devotions added a deeper dive as I studied Proverbs daily in month 2.

Step 3: December—I was finishing my first year and wanted to dive deeper, so I purchased a few more devotionals and a Bible Commentary on Proverbs, found in the Resources section.

Step 4: January 2020—I started reading the Commentary in addition to the devotionals and daily reading of a chapter in Proverbs. I was slowly immersing myself in the wisdom of Proverbs and the perspectives these Christian authors had gleaned.

Step 5: February 2021—I ordered the book "Studies in the Sermon on the Mount" by D. Martyn Lloyd-Jones, referenced in the Biblical Commentaries.

The author shared that the Sermon on the Mount which Jesus preached was likened to "Proverbs" of the New Testament. [1]

Step 6: March 23, 2021—The day after surgery, I pulled out the book, "Studies in the Sermon on the Mount," and started reading. I had packed my pens and highlighters, using them liberally as I learned so much as I read.

Step 7: June 2021—I invited some friends to read the first half of the book mentioned above and discuss what we were learning every week throughout the summer. We met weekly on my lanai, and our discussions were rich. The wisdom that God was unfolding as we studied together took us to new levels in our faith.

Step 8: January of 2022—I continue to study and add to the devotionals and commentaries that cover Proverbs. I have more to learn, and look forward to what God has in store for me as I continue to study His Word daily.

Wisdom

Do I think wisdom is only acquired by studying Proverbs? True wisdom is found in Proverbs, but there are 65 other books of the Bible to learn from, too. I have provided in this chapter and throughout this book a handful of ways I have used to acquire wisdom. There are many more out there. Each person has different learning styles and also has a distinct desire to learn and grow.

The first thing to consider would be, is pursuing wisdom where you are in your life?

- I was not aware of the distinction between wisdom and secular knowledge and have not considered pursuing a path of acquiring wisdom.
- My interest has been piqued after reading this section.
- I have been studying wisdom on a low level or occasionally.
- I am actively pursuing acquiring wisdom and have a plan to pursue it.

- I have been studying wisdom in The Bible on an ongoing basis and am possibly mentoring someone or others.

The next thing to consider is your learning style.

- Do you learn by:
  - Reading
  - Listening
  - Watching
  - Interactively

Do you have accessibility to books/podcasts/videos/mentors?

- Purchase
- Check out from the library
- Borrow from a friend or church

Do you have time in your schedule?

- Refer to Chapter 8

Now that you have reviewed these questions and answered them, you can make a plan that matches your desire and available time. You can utilize the resources in the back of this book and any suggested to you by those who have also been pursuing wisdom.

Prepare for a Shift

As you spend time consistently acquiring wisdom, you will start to notice changes. These changes will be noted in your mindset, attitude, faith, relationships, career, and more. It will be different for everyone as God has a unique plan for each of us. The impact of the wisdom acquired will ripple out and affect one, some, or many.

I didn't plan on writing a book when I started participating in Bible Studies and Proverbs. I knew there was a "tug" in my stomach to do something, but God didn't make it clear to me until the summer of 2021. I had a path of growth that was my own. Many years and growth in multiple areas brought me to where I am today. I also know that God is not finished with my growth plan. I don't know exactly where he will take me, but I am focused on Him and will continue to study and be obedient to His callings in my life.

Your growth path will be uniquely yours. What you study and when you study will be for reasons that God will reveal to you as you are ready to understand fully. As he unveils His plan for you, be obedient to His call. You won't be fully equipped. He will provide you with enough to guide you safely forward, step by step. Be prepared for some significant steps along the way. Some parts of our journeys will be faster than we thought, but it will be an essential part of our testimonies that we share as He asks us.

Can you imagine if you lean in to follow God's plan? What if ten people whom you know also gained wisdom and followed God's plan for their lives because you leaned in? How about 100 people in your community who followed God's calling because you leaned in to God's prompting? Can you imagine the ripple effect that will happen within our communities, our states, country, and the world? God wants His Word to be proclaimed to all, and each person who leans in will ultimately have an impact that will stretch further than we can imagine.

As I sat down to write this book, I prayed that it would impact at least one person. I know that sharing my cancer journey on social media last summer has already affected and changed the lives of multiple people. It humbles me to realize that. I am not a social media "influencer." However, our reach on social media or within our friend and family networks allows us to affect others. Use your platform as God encourages you to share the gifts of wisdom He is growing in you.

The most crucial point to embrace is a posture of humility and gratitude in this journey. I have learned so much from the Apostles in the New Testament.

Their lives leave us a living example and a humble peek into the roads they walked. The culture we live in shouts pride, me first, and entitlement, to name a few. The posture of "me first" is not what God wants us to pursue in the callings He asks us to complete. Matthew 6:3-4 NIV gives us pointed instruction: "But when you give to the needy, do not let your left hand know what your right hand is doing, so that your giving may be in secret." Our calling is not to exploit us. It is to glorify God.

With the calling of acquiring wisdom introduced, I pray that this is a point that you spend some time on in prayer. And as you pray, below are a few questions to journal, answer, and pray over.

SEEDS SOWN

Questions to Journal

Studying wisdom is general for a reason. We experience many different things each day, and learning in a broad focus is quite helpful as you pursue wisdom. Are you ready to embrace a more comprehensive and/or focused lens as you study?

Whom can you study with? Whom can you reach out to for further clarification as you learn?

How have you benefited in the past as you have studied a particular subject?

_____

_____

_____

_____

_____

_____

_____

_____

_____

_____

_____

_____

_____

_____

CHAPTER 5

A FAITH LIKE SWEET MISS DIAN'S—FAITHFUL MENTORS

"And let us consider how we may spur one another on toward
love and good deeds. Let us not give up meeting together,
as some are in the habit of doing but let us encourage one
another—and all the more as you see the Day approaching."

HEBREWS 10: 24-25 NIV

This part of my journey happened well before my diagnosis but leads to today, no matter what day you picked this book up to read it. God guides each step of our lives; and as I look back on our move to Florida from the Midwest, He orchestrated every detail that would impact the specific care I received during the most significant health diagnosis I have had to date.

The Neighborhood that is a Family

Let me take you back to the Summer of 2018. My husband, Art, received a job offer that would move us from a short stint in Indianapolis to our dream of living in Florida. He moved ahead of our kids and me. Along with starting a new job, he became our on-the-ground home shopper. Not only did he have to look at many houses, but also we had to put in more offers on houses than we ever had before. And they all fell through for various reasons. We put our belongings in PODS and sent them to storage. Then I drove to Florida with our kids to join my husband before finding the house we now live in. Our realtor called me as we were just south of Atlanta on a Saturday morning, squealing with delight. "I found your home!!!" And she had. That weekend we walked through the house we would sign on to purchase. The long search turned into a whirlwind closing of a home sale, and we were so relieved.

We hoped the neighbors were friendly; that was always our prayer as we moved throughout our marriage. We have had many wonderful neighbors, but our current street is not just your ordinary neighborhood. We soon found our Florida family residing in the houses that fill our street. Meeting them and being welcomed into the neighborhood family didn't take long. We weren't the ones who formed the family of our street, but they lovingly grafted us into the family tree.

My husband is a senior leader at an artisanal corporate bakery, and the loaves of bread/pastries they make are nothing short of phenomenal. I asked him to bring home a few loaves of garlic bread. We decided this was a straightforward way to make friends with our new neighbors. Who doesn't love bread with a meal? We knew we had a way to everyone's heart with this gift.

With fresh garlic bread, packaged individually in Ziploc bags, I set out to knock on doors and introduce myself. I started at the last home on the street and rang the doorbell. Strange, no answer. I am pretty sure I saw their car in the driveway. So, I started walking away from their door, and the gal across the street yelled my way—"They don't answer the front door; go around to the side door." I smiled and shared that I would drop by soon.

As I made my way to the side door and rang that doorbell, the sweetest woman opened the door and greeted me…a tad surprised by the stranger holding some loaves of bread. I smiled and quickly introduced myself. I wanted to extend an introduction. Fully dressed and with make-up applied, she introduced herself, with a beautiful Southern accent, as Dian. I soon learned these details were her trademark. She is a true Southern lady in every sense of the word. As our relationship grew, I added a few adjectives to her name, and I now affectionately refer to her as Sweet Miss Dian. She shared that her husband's name was Bill. We exchanged pleasantries, and I let her go.

As I walked away from Bill and Dian's home, their next-door neighbor was in his front yard. I quickly walked over, introduced myself to him, and learned his name was Conway. I admired the tall concrete walls surrounding his property, and I could see many trees peeking over. We quickly launched into a lengthy conversation and discovered we both had worked in medical careers. We both enjoyed gardening. Conway provided me with an impromptu but detailed tour of his backyard garden. I was speechless. As a midwesterner, I knew I had much to learn about gardening in Florida. I filed away the many details he shared that day, but most importantly, that he was a retired anesthesiologist. Our relationship would be an essential connection in the exceptional care I would be given as I received my diagnosis. We quickly became friends as he shared his produce as much as we shared the bread my husband continued to bring home.

As I knocked on everyone's door and greeted the neighbors with loaves of fresh bread, I shared with them that they had access to more fresh bread when they wanted. We have sixteen homes on our cul-de-sac; and within a few days, I met them all. I was getting a glimpse into the families of our neighborhood with each introduction I made. Everyone was excited to have a new family move in, and they were open to getting to know us better.

You share your backyard fence with two, sometimes three, families, which can be an excellent thing or a point of contention. Each family that we share a fence with is entirely genuine. As you can guess by the descriptions, we love each of our "fence" neighbors. One of our "fence neighbors" are John and Carllyn. They are the sweetest and most caring couple and have learned that if their door is left open, Andy, our dog, will welcome himself into their home.

When I met our other next-door neighbor, Jessica, it was a quick conversion from new neighbors to friends and soon-to-be best friends. Her eyes were full of joy, she had that Southern accent that won my heart in a beat, and she was in yoga gear. I was pretty sure this was going in the right direction. We found many similarities, and the love of our dogs was just the tip of the iceberg. More to come on our relationship as this chapter unfolds.

Walking Andy and Being Grafted into Our Neighborhood Family

There are many beautiful things about Florida, but my favorite is that there are 365 great weather days to walk our dog, Andy. To say I was ecstatic NEVER to have to walk in the snow or minus 40-degree winter days that we experienced in the 15 winters we lived in the Minneapolis area was not an understatement. Andy and I walk twice a day. I saw our neighbors frequently as I walked by their homes, and we all enjoyed getting to know each other in these quick but frequent chats. As they shared more details about this street, I quickly discovered that this neighborhood had a history; and it was terrific. I was quietly blown away by each conversation I had with each neighbor and learned more about the families who started and have lived on our charming street in paradise for its length of existence.

My kids would shake their heads as I shared what I learned through the many conversations and the great relationships I was making with everyone on this street. They nicknamed me "Nosy Nancy"...the only minor detail is that I rarely asked any probing questions in the conversations with our neighbors.

These kind and beautiful people shared little details of life on our street. They were sharing the information about this neighborhood just as you would if you were welcoming a newly-married family member into your family. It turns out that homes on this street rarely go for sale; and 55+ years later, there are three original owners, and most people have lived here for 40-50 years. A handful of others have been here more than 10+ years, and the last few of us are newer over the previous five years. It is also not unusual for family members of the next generation to move in as their parents pass away.

I am not sharing this to spill "gossip." I am sharing this to help you understand how forming relationships with those around you can change your neighborhood into a family. As I said, we have lived in multiple homes; and our first neighborhood in Eden Prairie, Minnesota, was pretty close to this good. We called them family, too. It is true that when you come out of your house, look around, and say more than just "hi" to your neighbor, the dynamics change in your relationship with your neighbors. The connections go from describing your neighbors as so and so who lives in the white house to knowing them well enough to text/call and know they will reply/answer instantly. You are never "ghosted" in this neighborhood. We will drop everything and run for whatever reason, especially if a snake is involved! It creates an atmosphere of a family—love, hope, and peace—which you immediately feel as you pull onto our street.

Let Me Paint the Picture

I share the length of time that some families have lived on this street to emphasize that our feelings and experiences are not unique. The original owners started this "family" from our street's beginnings. Sweet Miss Dian and her husband were the first to purchase their lot on our street. The four-lane road that runs by our street was a dirt road in the mid-1960s. This neighborhood was part of some farmers' orchards and pasture land. The road outside of our street is named after his family. These intimate details warm my heart to its core. It creates a sense of more than just mere home ownership. It has created a stronger bond than any legal term could describe.

Sweet Miss Dian has shared many memories of how our street filled in with families through the years and how the kids played throughout the years as they grew up. She has shared who moved in and how each family fits into the network of this neighborhood family. She has also shared about where they are now. I intend to write down all these details of our neighborhood history to preserve for future generations.

One detail that intrigues me as a nurse is that this street has a steep history in the hospital, where I eventually received care. Our street has been the home address of many doctors and their families. They have also inspired their children to follow in their careers. These men have significantly impacted the health and lives of many people in this community. I feel a little in awe of those who have lived here before us. To me, it is a high standard to carry on and an honor to carry on their legacy in our unique way.

Sweet Miss Dian told me that Conway had put all of us to sleep on this street. And she said that her late husband, Bill, would always tag onto that with, "He always woke us all up, too." There are so many more details she has shared about the surgeons who have taken personal care of the neighbors here. It is incredible to hear the details of comfort and care that have happened over the years because of these friendships formed here. Our hospital has a great ad campaign that features pictures or a quick word of comfort from their staff; and as I have learned the names of the previous residents on this street, I smile as I see them in these commercials. These doctors have and continue to provide life-changing care.

Another part of our neighborhood family is Tom and Sandy, who reside across the street from us. If you know my parents, it's like living right across the street from them. They are genuinely the sweetest couple! The conversations we have are rooted in our faith in Christ. I sit like a student when we chat on their couch or in their driveway because the wisdom they share in each conversation is golden. Again, they don't set out to teach as they talk, but each conversation we have has a life-changing takeaway. And like good neighbors, they always have room in their refrigerator or freezer if my pan doesn't fit in ours. Of course, I always leave a few pieces behind for them to eat.

Mentor Moments

I have been blessed to have many mentors throughout the years. I count each of my extended family in one way or the other as one. And as I have grown, my mentors have ebbed and flowed as we have moved; but a few I am going to take a moment to share with you so you can get to know them. And these insights may help you as you connect with a mentor for yourself.

Deb

"Two are better than one, because they have a good return for their labor: If either of them falls, one can help the other up," Ecclesiastes 4:9-10 NIV.

"Aunt Deb" is a term that I gave to my best friend I met in college after giving birth to our oldest son. Deb and I met as we started chatting after one of our Animal Biology classes our sophomore year at the University of Iowa. We found out we were heading back to the same dorm and ended up chatting the whole way there. We have not stopped talking since then! We soon learned that we have almost identical family dynamics and upbringing. Our relationship has felt like finding the twin you were separated from at birth. We have a special bond and a relationship that has enriched our lives to this day. We have experienced it all together even though I have moved away from her and all over the country. We attended special events and visited each other as much as we could through the years. We have encouraged each other when we felt a bit unprepared for whatever was being thrown at us, and we knew the other would just listen and hear the other one out. We celebrated to the max in all the good times.

Mentors add to your life in different ways. Mentors grow together, always helping each other get better. No matter the distance between you, they add to all the good times, are present with you in the rough seasons, and help you "see" the road ahead that looks blurry to you in the present. They are always "present," no matter their geographical location. Take notice of those in your life who help light your path with each encouraging conversation.

Jessica

Jessica is my Florida neighbor and best friend. She has become priceless in my life and way more than someone I can call in a pinch if I need an ingredient for my cooking. I can't remember how we decided to start walking our dogs every Sunday morning, but that's what started our relationship. When we started, she had two boxers, Nala and Luna, but added a handsome lab, Ollie. I have Andy, a Goldendoodle. And we decided that we could commit to that day as we shared our schedules. On these walks, each Sunday, our relationship formed and became ours entirely. Her family had moved in about a year before we did, and she had found some neighborhoods perfect for dog walking. These weren't short adventures. We started walking "Long Bow" to begin with, about 3.6 miles, and have progressed to our usual 6.4-mile walk on "Kent." I soon learned that the details, the length and pace, became an important detail of our Sunday walks. Jessica is an avid exerciser, and has inspired me to step up my exercise game. I will leave those details for a later spot in this book.

Our weekly walks are filled with lively conversations as we share what had happened in our lives before we met. Jessica and I grew up in different parts of the country, and our families and life experiences have impacted our lives as we mature. We converse about our families, our careers, health/wellness, and every detail of current events. We pretty much know all the details of our lives. We connected deeply and continue to hold these conversations as a protected part of our relationship. These life experiences we brought to our relationship have helped us each want to learn more from each other and grow to be even better. These weekly walks soon became a non-negotiable part of our lives.

Conversations with mentors are authentic, make us think more profoundly, and encourage us to evaluate the next steps of our lives. We may not intentionally set up mentor relationships. Jessica and I didn't set out to be mentors to each other. We just wanted to be friends. Take notice of your relationships causing you to improve in one or more areas. One of your friends can unexpectedly become a mentor if you observe the pearls of wisdom they share. These relationships are the ones that will change the trajectory of your life. Mentors help us "level up" in one or multiple areas.

Karyn

Karyn and I work at the same company, but we've never met because we live in different states and work remotely. Karyn and I have seen each other for quite a while on Zoom screens, but it wasn't until my diagnosis that our relationship began to form. Karyn reached out with a picture of flowers and a note beside them that said—Pray for Ann. She continues to send an updated picture of flowers each week in my private messages on our work instant messaging system. As a gardener, this gives me another reason to want to visit her. I was appreciative of the thoughtfulness the first time. And blown away each week they came. The weekly pictures started a dialogue. We shared more of each other, and more prayer requests were shared from each of us. At this point, the bond of our friendship was anchored. And one day, a package from Karyn arrived in my mailbox. It was the most beautiful book I have ever seen. The artwork was meticulous, and the message in between the beautiful pictures provided rest to my weary heart amid my cancer treatment. The images continue to arrive each week in the instant notifications of our work instant messaging system, and we have sweet conversations in between.

Mentors reach out and shine a light. They encourage, lift us up, and shine a ray of hope. Sometimes, they accomplish this with pictures of flowers and a note that says, "Praying for Ann." Mentors can achieve so much with a thoughtful message and a prayer offered.

Duane and Jill

Duane and Jill. This couple has wrapped their marriage together in a love that endures and has always pointed us to our Savior, Jesus. I met Jill as I was added as a leader to the BSF leadership group. As part of my introduction, I shared that we had moved from Minneapolis via Indy, and there was an immediate connection. Jill had lived in a suburb of Minneapolis at different points in her early life. If you have lived in Minnesota at any point in your life, you know this fact. Once a Minnesotan, always a Minnesotan. You are joined at the hip as long as you have an address with a zip code that starts with 55XXX. And the accent you acquire in your time there lingers no matter where you move.

The times we have spent with Duane and Jill are countless and fruitful. They never have an "agenda" as you would expect from mentors, but I have always gleaned multiple nuggets which enhance many areas of our lives just through conversation and being in their presence. One of their gifts is hospitality. They have opened their home to us for many meals or the ability just to drop by. And they have been generous in introducing us to additional friends of theirs along the way. Another "gift" they have is their marriage. They are one of a handful of couples, I can honestly say, who have taken the vow of two becoming one seriously and beautifully. And this is something that is rare and encouraging in a culture that throws marriage and masculinity by the wayside daily. Becoming "one" in marriage is continually worked at, and it shows how diligently they have worked to become "one." From every word that comes out as they talk to the actions observed as they interact, their marriage is the sweetest and most valuable gift from God to observe, take home, and apply.

Another gift they have is creating deep relationships with each generation of their family. Not only are they dedicated in their marriage, but also with their grown children and their grandchildren. Everyone in their family is loved and cared for through the deep relationships they created with each child and grandchild. How precious it is to make each relationship in our family a high priority. They are teaching everyone around them many steps and ideas to create bonds that are deep and valued by all generations.

Most mentors like Duane and Jill can impact your life in all areas. They will "laugh" as they read this because they will probably think, we are just friends. We aren't trying to teach you anything. I am a student of Godly ways to live each time we are together. And maybe that's a point we need to be aware of as we interact with others. We need to be observant in all situations for many reasons, but mostly how we can learn from our relationships with others. How do those we spend time with positively affect our actions, choices, and ultimately our marriages? High-quality mentors' ways are to be applied. Don't just observe; implement.

Susie

I want to share about my lifelong mentor. It's my sister, Susie. She has been stuck with me for most of her life. I rudely entered her life when she was four years old. When we were growing up, we did a lot of things together—our farm chores, walking beans, 4-H demonstrations, and our mom also dressed us alike, too on some occasions. As most siblings back in the day, we were privileged to share a bedroom. Lucky for her, we even shared a bed. Because I was a restless sleeper, I was a disaster to sleep with at night. And the stories of my whining when I was younger are legendary among our family. I was not the child that was seen and not heard. Everyone knew I was around. So, as we grew up and because of the age difference of 4 years, my sister was not thrilled to spend much time with me. Fair enough.

But things changed after I graduated from college, and we started to have more similarities in our lives—we both were married and having kids. Instead of my being the tag along and complaining about everything, we now had husbands and kids that bonded us very closely. Our relationship was completely transforming into the closest kinship. Through the years, we have listened as we have shared great things that have happened, struggles that have surfaced within our family, progress on our goals we are pursuing, and all surrounding our faith journeys. Sometimes we have given feedback and suggestions, and we have prayed emergently. We were always there for each other, and we have grown because we have always encouraged each other to stretch to be better. We knew God had a bigger purpose for our lives, even though the purpose was sometimes immediately unclear.

As the information became clear that I had a real problem with my health the last few years, we got raw and honest with each other and leaned on our faith to levels we had never done before. We would cry together at the slight but real possibility that this cancer would take my life. We talked about the difficulties that may come, and she volunteered to drop everything and come whenever I needed her. We prayed a lot. We would share Scripture verses that were giving us comfort. And sometimes, we just chatted about anything to make our time on the phone last a little bit longer. But more importantly, she kept asking me questions about what I was learning from my care team. She understood I was not just going along for the ride during my treatment. Susie saw the active steps I was taking to work hand in hand with God's healing of my body. She asked good questions when some actions I was taking or considering seemed a little more advanced than what she thought I should do. I noted this attention to detail and feedback.

This journey challenged us in many areas of our life, including our health. We were determined to make even better choices than we had so far. We have shared recipes that included options to increase the nutrients in our food choices and have introduced them to our families. We encourage each other with our exercise/activity levels. Whatever we learned, we shared and grew our knowledge levels together.

And as I shared earlier, Susie and her husband were the brave ones who stated the obvious. Ann, you need to write a book. That's another fundamental part of mentoring others. You take the precise moment when it is open and encourage those you are mentoring to take the path God has laid out for them.

Mentoring relationships can work both ways. Each of you becomes a mentor of the other person. The path of our life may look more treacherous at some points. Life will make you learn/grow in ways you may not think you are ready for. Mentors help with the transformation in your life. They allow you to see around the corner you are about to turn. And because they have some additional knowledge to what you have, they prepare you for some of the bumps that may come up. Mentors have traveled further than you and can help light your path a bit further than you could initially see. Be open to being a mentor and a mentee in the same relationship. There is a great scripture—"Iron sharpens iron." Susie and I may not think we are sharpening each other, but we are. And I am very thankful for the sister she continues to be for me.

Sweet Miss Dian

And now, to share my mentoring relationship with Sweet Miss Dian. As you have read thus far, all my chapter titles have been about faithful men in the Bible. As you read this chapter title, most of you were thinking, there is no mention of a Dian in the Bible. Dian is my neighbor and not in the Bible. If you have studied the Bible for any length of time, you know that God used many women to accomplish His plan. He equipped women in many ways to rise to their moment, and rise they did. As I have gotten to know Sweet Miss Dian, I see many ways God has equipped her and has raised her up on many occasions.

You won't read about her in the local magazines which feature the "in" people in the "Who's Who" section of our coastal beach paradise. She lived her life for God, not for worldly fame. Trust me, she and her husband were humble "giants" in our community long before we moved to town. I have heard stories of their contributions from the most unusual sources. But they weren't about the spotlight. They magnified God and loved this community in ways that bring me to tears as I type.

How did my relationship with Dian go from a neighbor across the street to Sweet Miss Dian? A few things happened beyond chatting as I walked Andy by her home each day. My sister visited me shortly after Dian's husband passed away. Susie and I had decided we needed a fun lunch at a fun beach spot. I knew just the location and asked my sister if she minded if we invited Dian to go with us. I thought Dian might need a little time out for a pick-me-up with some girls. Susie readily agreed as I shared bits and pieces about Sweet Miss Dian in our conversations.

The fun began when she hopped in my car and said, "Let's case the joint!" My sister looked at me and said, "Who is she?!" I smiled from ear to ear and said, "Do you understand now why I love her??!!" Did I mention that she is over 80 years old and running around as quickly as I am?? I backed out of her drive, and we were off to lunch at "The Don," a local beach hotel with a long, opulent history. The setting was breathtaking, the food was incredible, and our conversation reflected our deepening relationships. Time spent with Sweet Miss Dian is never unforgettable. She is witty. She is wise. She speaks with a passion that draws your attention to her voice—but points straight to Jesus. And if you are paying attention and actively filing away what she is sharing, your life will be enriched forever and entirely changed.

The next part that led us closer than we anticipated was the result of a hot water leak into our foundation after a leak in our kitchen. We found ourselves without hot water in our home until we could fix the overall plumbing problem. Ummmm, I don't do cold showers. And Sweet Miss Dian agreed. Without hesitation, she immediately said I was welcome to shower at her home until we fixed our overall plumbing problem. I was stunned and beyond grateful. And with all honesty, several neighbors offered us the same thing. But there was something in her invitation that I couldn't say no to.

I didn't want to impose daily, but that changed quickly. Two days after my first shower, I received a text from Sweet Miss Dian that said, "Are you clean enough?!" She knew I couldn't go too long in the Florida heat without a shower. She knew I needed to clean up sooner rather than later. I gathered my shower supplies together and walked over to take my shower. These sweet texts became our routine to "schedule" my showers. She never missed putting a smile on my face with her quick wit in her text messages. The Saturday texts are my favorite—"Are you clean enough for church?" Occasionally, I would manage to text her first to schedule my shower time.

It turns out that when you frequently shower at someone's home, it is more than just a few minutes popping in to take a shower, especially at Sweet Miss Dian's. It often involved a conversation about what was happening in our lives and generally commenced after I showered and found her at her table working on her Bible Study. I would casually sit in one of her chairs and these endearing conversations commenced. And these talks took on so many insightful directions. She was studying Proverbs when this routine started. That is one of my favorite books of the Bible to study, and we talked at length about what we have learned as we studied Proverbs. The conversations would then move to her sharing sweet memories of growing up in Baton Rouge, her family, how she met Bill, and the memories of living in our neighborhood. These conversations deepened as this routine continued. Something was uniquely different about our interactions. I felt a shift. As we talked, I felt more like a student, not just a neighbor. She was passing on wisdom with each conversation we had. She was sharing a piece of her faithful legacy with me, but why? God soon revealed that to both of us.

Following this revelation, I flashed back to my diagnosis. And I remembered how many people "leaned in" to love on us in their way. I had a moment when I thought I should probably not continue to shower at Dian's, but she insisted that

I continue. I knew that was my way to "lean in" and be present with her at this time. And "lean in" I did. God blessed those times abundantly.

There was one evening that stood out to me. I had arrived for my usual shower, and Dian's daughter, Paula, greeted me at the side door. I went in and hopped in the shower. After I had finished my shower, I found Dian and Paula sitting down for dinner; and they asked me to chat as they ate. I can't ever say no to Sweet Miss Dian. So I sat down. We all reached out our hands to pray together. Dian led the prayer. Each petition she said to God grabbed my heart a little deeper, and I shed a few tears. Her faith is so real because she knows Jesus so profoundly and intimately. Her prayers are easy conversations with her best friend. Each moment with Dian is a reminder to know Jesus more personally each day.

On occasion, I grab a shower after my walk with Andy. This morning, Dian was not feeling very well; but her daughter, Julie, knew the routine and welcomed me in. I showered and checked in to have her give my regards to Dian. Julie looked at me and said, "She wants you to come into her room and talk." I quietly entered her room, and she opened her eyes and invited me to sit in the chair next to her. I nestled into the armchair, knowing this was not a quick chat. She quietly started the conversation, and the wisdom just flowed. I listened intently as usual. I never know what I will learn, but the mental notes I take each conversation are lengthy. She is purposeful in these conversations. And I am one of the many in her life who have been granted the gift of being her "student."

Like my friends Duane and Jill, Sweet Miss Dian and her late husband, Bill, have a high priority on their relationships with their daughters. But the relationships with their grandchildren have become a loving focus since their birth! And not only their relationships, but sharing their faith in Jesus and Jesus' great love for their grandchildren. In every interaction they have had with these phenomenal kids, Bill and Dian always let Jesus shine. What a privilege I have had as Dian has shared so many memories of the times with each grandchild. As they watched each grandchild flourish in a particular area, Bill and Dian placed their activities around that grandchild's strength. They poured into this next generation of their family to lovingly wrap them in an extra layer of love. What a legacy they have created for each generation!

As I described earlier, Dian's prayer life is one to model. Her deepest desire is that her grandchildren will not miss out on the gift of heaven. It's been said that our Grandmother's prayers are still protecting each of us and being answered. Prayers don't stop just because our loved one may be in heaven. Their prayers they have prayed throughout their lives can and will be answered for generations to come. Just like the promise and covenant given to Abraham by God to make his descendants as numerous as the stars in the sky, our prayers can have an impact on our family's generations to come. That is Sweet Miss Dian's prayer for her grandchildren—that each will know Jesus as their Savior and experience the gift of eternal life. This prayer is one that I hope each of us pray for our families and the generations to come.

Most evenings, I walk home with my clothes wrapped in my towel in awe of how God built our relationship due to a water leak. He truly makes all things beautiful. And our relationship has changed my life. The fruits of our relationship will last far beyond both of our earthly lives. God works the details of all areas of our lives like that. God is paving the way for what is developing in the relationship between Dian and me to go on. And on. In its own unique way, it will change the world.

The Impact of Mentors

Throughout our life, everyone we spend time with impacts our life. Our family, friends, teachers, coaches, and business colleagues are some examples of these relationships. These interactions can be positive or negative. In some relationships, like our family, we don't have a choice in our association. In most relationships, we can choose how much time we spend with those people. We may not think right away about how each relationship is mentoring us, but it is.

We have the responsibility and the choice of with whom our time is spent. Bringing this awareness into more focus will change the trajectory of our lives for the better. Our mentors will come to us in two paths—intentional and unintentional. There will be points in our lives where we realize that we want to move in a better direction, and we will seek out people who will teach us the things we need to learn to move us in the correct direction. Other people will be brought into our lives by God. He will place people in our lives that we weren't planning on, and they will impact our lives and set us on a course to help us grow to a level we may not have anticipated.

We need to be more attentive to the availability of mentors. Throughout our life, we will be presented with options that will either make our life path better or worse. If we are connected with quality mentors, we will be prepared when opportunities are presented, and we will be able to make better choices. Each better choice is a choice that impacts everyone more positively. As we look at the next generation watching us, it is a teaching moment for them each time we make the optimal choice. It is another reminder that our choices matter, and we are "teaching" with each decision we make. Others are watching. Make it a life worth duplicating.

The thought may be crossing your mind, how do I find a mentor? Here is a question that I have found helpful in creating the opportunity to grow your network of friends and mentors—Who do you know that I should get to know? People you know or are getting to know due to a move or new career move will help you connect. You need to ask. People enjoy helping others; and when you are genuine with your inquiries, you will be amazed at who they will make a mutual introduction to.

The next level of mentoring is called a Mastermind Group. Creating a Mastermind Group is a great way to gather 3+ people with common overarching goals of improvement in their lives. They each bring different strengths to the gatherings. During their time together, the members will share ideas and obstacles; and their conversations are solution oriented. The purpose of this group is to challenge each other to move to the next level in their lives—leadership, parenting, education, faith, etc. The subject area is specific to each group and may morph as the group moves forward in its journey.

How do you form a Mastermind Group? Pray and ask God to lead you to the people with whom He would want you to gather. It will be a mixed group at the beginning of knowledge of each other. Usually, you will know 1 or 2 of the members, and they will invite 1 or 2 members that would add value to the group. When you form or join a Mastermind Group, be ready for the shift that will happen in your life. God's plan is unfolding, and he will prepare us for the leap we will be taking.

Christian mentors have an additional impact. They point you to the most crucial relationship, your relationship with Jesus. I found this quote on social media and equated this to all the talks I had, especially with my sister during my journey.

"To my sister who thinks that it's over because she's facing a seemingly unbeatable giant…Keep in mind that impossible is where God starts, and miracles are what He does," Girls Just Pray Ministries. [1]

This quote struck me to the core regarding Christian mentors. My sister and other Christian mentors in my life literally would speak the Word of God over me in our conversations and as we prayed. When our mentors are always in God's Word, their guidance is solid to the core. And their direction will always point us to the Scriptures written by God. That solid truth that guides the mentors in our lives is what we long for and can grow the most from. Our time on earth is meant for God to transform us to be more like Jesus every day so that when we, as believers, walk into heaven, we are transformed into our perfect new bodies.

My sister, when her daughter Emma was born, found a hymn she wanted to be sung by the men in our family at Emma's baptism. It has become a special memory that we insert at the most significant markers in our family's lives—baptisms, confirmations, funerals, etc. The song, "I Was There to Hear Your Borning Cry," points to specific life moments of our faith journey and how

God is faithful throughout. I want to close this chapter with a favorite verse from the hymn, as Sweet Miss Dian is no longer praying to Jesus from earth; she has closed her weary eyes and is walking with Him in heaven. Until we walk with Jesus and you in heaven Sweet Miss Dian…

> *In the middle ages of your life, not too old, no longer young,*
> *I'll be there to guide you through the night, complete what I've begun.*
> *When the evening gently closes in, and you shut your weary eyes,*
> *I'll be there as I have always been with just one more surprise.*
> *I was there to hear your borning cry, I'll be there when you are old.*
> *I rejoiced the day you were baptized, to see your life unfold.* [2]

The numbers of our earthly days are known only to God; enjoy each day that you have with your mentors. The days and the moments with Sweet Miss Dian have changed my life. Because of Dian, I will live with more intention each day that I am here on earth.

Questions to Journal

How could you see a mentor making a more significant difference in your life?

Make a list of people you currently see as mentors in your life. Jot down by their name how they are mentoring you. After completing this, ask yourself if there are any additional areas you need mentoring in? Pray for God to open up a relationship that will turn into mentoring in your area of need.

Do you mentor anyone? If so, or if not, pray that God will equip you with whom to mentor and how to mentor them.

_____

_____

_____

_____

_____

_____

_____

_____

_____

_____

_____

_____

CHAPTER 6

INTENTION—WE NEED AN ADVOCATE

"And I will ask the Father, and he will give you another Counselor, to be with you forever—the Spirit of truth."

JOHN 14:16-17a NIV

We all have advocates in our lives. We have people who will defend us, speak up for us, and also look out for our well-being. And we return the advocacy to others throughout our life. It is a special spot in someone's life when you take on the role of advocate. Sometimes we step in for the youngest of children that have been abandoned at such a young and vulnerable age. And sometimes we step in at the end of someone's life to assure that they are protected and safe, their dignity is preserved, and they are well cared for. It is part of our value system to protect others. And when some are left without an advocate, they are left vulnerable and open to bad effects. In this world, we have a broken advocacy system. Some people fall through the cracks, and others are left with gaps in the care they receive because they are not sure how to ask for the correct help.

Surrounded by a Family of Advocates

My family plans everything. We are all about celebrating milestones of accomplishments together. This fact means my dad's 80th birthday and my parents 55th wedding anniversary became an event to attend within weeks of each other. Only a significant illness/diagnosis would be acceptable to miss. And technically, my cancer diagnosis fits into that category. My sister-in-law lovingly said, "Ann, we would rather celebrate all the other events WITH you than you risk traveling for this." And technically, she was correct. But, I don't like missing out on anything with our family. A sense of FOMO—Fear of Missing Out—has a deep-seated pull from the bottom of my heart.

Round 7 of chemo was on August 2, 2021, and the party was on the weekend following. I had already dropped the idea with my care team early on. They always looked at me and gave me stern advice that travel is not advised; but IF your labs are ok, we will let you go. As a nurse, I watched my labs EACH and EVERY treatment week. My labs have remained stable the whole time so far, making my care team very pleased and hopeful for my care plan. I always planned to buy my plane tickets as soon as my labs were back on August 2nd and my chemo was infused. I wasn't going to miss their party. And so, that Monday afternoon, I purchased plane tickets for myself and our kids; and we flew out to Iowa later that week. The other reason I wanted to travel was to see my husband. He could drive quickly from his spot in Wisconsin to my parents to celebrate and see me. It was a massive win on all accounts.

Our entire family was there. We had some new additions and made introductions. And as per our usual family traditions, things went as planned. Memorable songs, prayers, and fellowship abounded the whole weekend. So many came to celebrate our parents, and many were surprised and happy to see me doing so well amid my treatment. I also received some sweet encouragement from a few members of our community who had been through the same diagnosis and were thriving. Those stories lit an additional fire of belief in me to continue strong for the last half when I returned home.

The kids and I flew back to Florida on Monday. Things changed on Tuesday. I woke up not feeling well, but I worked the day anyhow. The aches, the exhaustion, and most likely, I was starting to spike a fever on Wednesday or Thursday. Like any good nurse, I had lost the thermometer in one of our moves. I needed to shower one of those mornings, but I was super weak. I knew that if I fell while I was taking a shower, my dog couldn't dial 9-1-1. So, I called my sister, put her on speaker phone, and talked to her the whole time. Let's just insert here that it should have been a clue to call my doctor and be seen, but again, nurses are not very good patients. Friday rolled around, and I thought, I am going to get a liter of fluid at the infusion center. That will make this all turn around. I drove there and back and probably should have had a neighbor drive me. But after the added fluids, I did feel a little bit better that afternoon.

And then Saturday came. I did not feel well at all. I asked my kids to purchase a thermometer. When they arrived home, I put it in my mouth, and it beeped. 103.1 degrees Fahrenheit. That is not good! I looked at my kids and told them I needed to be driven to the hospital. I knew for sure they were going to admit me. I had cancer and a high temp, and COVID—delta strain was making its rounds. I knew my fate. I also knew that they had banned visitors from the hospitals. Crap. No one could come and make sure I was receiving good care. As bad as I felt, I knew I had to keep my nursing brain in gear. I had to do the best I could in my weakened state to be my own advocate in the hospital. If you remember, there was not a lot of positive news coming out of hospitals at that time if you were admitted with COVID.

So, I went to the ER. I had a hooded sweatshirt on, sweatpants and brought my blanket to stay warm. I was cold on a good day, and with a high temperature, I was shivering and freezing above my average. The admitting nurse, complete with her N-95 mask, looked at me with a direct stare as I shared with her that I had cancer, I had traveled via airplane, and now was sick. In addition, I had been around numerous people at the grocery stores and other big box stores where I had recently shopped. Still, there were some bad attitudes when you mentioned "air travel." She was less than pleased that I had not been vaccinated, either. A quick reminder here that we all do our due diligence for all medical decisions. One of the educational FAQs in my chemotherapy medication explanation explicitly stated not to receive immunizations while on chemotherapy because your immune system is suppressed. What choices you make in this time frame are entirely up to you, and I respect them.

As you can guess, our ER was packed; and there were many of us sitting in chairs awaiting our time to be seen as beds in the ER slowly opened up. I sent a selfie to my sister curled up with my hoodie over my head and my mask on—she forever calls me her COVID wookie. It took 6 hours to get an ER room and to be seen by a doctor in the ER. I finally consented to a COVID test. I had had 3 of them before with my surgeries and was no fan of the discomfort that came with them. Well, it came back with no doubt. I had COVID. The questions came like bullets as they tried to pinpoint where I got it. Well, I traveled with my mask on and was in contact with many people on airplanes and at "home." No one verbally told me they had COVID, so I cannot pinpoint precisely where I contracted it. I was more concerned about a plan to make me better than pointing a finger at who gave COVID to me.

They started an IV which is always a good thing when you are sick. Keeping a body hydrated makes a world of difference. The hospital was out of rooms, so I was given a hospital bed in my ER room for the night and most of the next day. I don't remember a lot, except that I was thankful they had installed a toilet right next to the cabinet in this room. And thankfully, nobody walked in while I was using it. Talk about losing your modesty. I was in no shape to take more than a step out of bed to use the bathroom. I knew I was in a world of hurt. I don't think they gave me anything for my fever, either. As a nurse, I was trying my best to figure out the plan of care they had established for COVID patients, and it looked pretty bleak in my semi-conscious state.

Late Sunday afternoon, I was moved up to a patient room; they mentioned that I would be on the 6th floor. And I was ecstatic, as that was the floor I was on to recover after my surgery. Those nurses were fantastic, and I was super encouraged! But then reality set in. It was not the same nurses, and the care was completely different. I was quickly becoming aware of what the Lepers in the Bible experienced. I was appalled. I have taken care of patients that had highly contagious illnesses. I knew how to isolate myself to protect myself as a nurse. And I never treated those patients like I was being treated on this admission.

After they had put me in my room, I went to the bathroom; and like any good nurse, I watched the color of my urine. It was getting darker—a sure sign of dehydration. I had awakened a few times so far and noticed my IV had "run dry" and was not always replaced as quickly as it should have been or at all. I then dragged myself and my IV pole out into the halls. I knew I had to walk. That is in the first chapter of patients recovering well. Get them out of their beds and make them walk. Keep their lungs open. Make them cough. The basics of nursing care never leave your mind, and came to mine, especially now when I was sicker than ever. I knew the things I had to do. BUT, a nurse at the nurse's station barked at me, "Get back to your room! You're going to get everyone sick!" I think I may have given her the same dirty look as I had previously given my surgeon. This time it was because I knew this wasn't right. I had my mask on, and if they work, who am I going to get sick? And also, I was pretty sure everyone on this unit had the same thing I did. I dragged myself and my IV pole back to my bed and literally collapsed.

A doctor awakened me. He introduced himself as the Infectious Disease doctor and was making rounds that evening. And I thought to myself; this poor guy probably has not been home in months. He is overworked and probably beyond sick of this situation. However, in the few moments that I remember, he told me that he would write an order for Regeneron and wait for approval from the insurance company. Again, in my stupor, I knew that I had researched Regeneron and knew that this one was working and not causing long-term problems for those with COVID. And because of a miracle of God, it was approved quickly, and they hung it within a few hours. I knew this was excellent news for me.

I couldn't help at this point craving the presence of my husband, my sister, or my neighbor, Conway. When you are sick, you need a visitor who will be your advocate—not one who will just sit there for entertainment. You need a coherent person who can call the right people for backup and credible information and ask for help when you are too weak. I was definitely in that place. I was too weak to call for help when I saw my dry IVs. I looked up at them and thought to myself, those are dry. They should be hanging a new one. Isn't anyone paying attention that I am not taking any fluids in by drinking? I knew they weren't keeping track of my urine output. So, I knew they were missing some critical assessment points in my care. Basic intake and output can tell a lot about a person's health status, and I knew I was behind. So, I prayed. I did have my cell phone with me and would video message my husband and my sister twice a day, so they knew I was alive. I never thought I would get worse because I have overall good health. But I knew they weren't doing much to improve me. I fully relied on the Holy Spirit to be my advocate as I was "alone" as a patient that weekend. And He fully was my unseen, but fully present, advocate.

The following day, a male voice awakened me. I remembered that voice. And I woke up and said, "Paul?" And he replied, "I thought it was you." He was the nurse educator on the floor and had come to give me discharge instructions. I was glad to converse with him because he knew his stuff. I was shocked that they were releasing me because I wasn't that much better, but I was in no shape to make a fuss. And shortly after he reviewed my information, I called our son to pick me up; and when he did, I was never so happy to see him and our dog.

I went home and collapsed into my bed. I started on a strict regimen of Tylenol to keep my fever down. I tried to eat some fruit-based popsicles to restart my hydration. I didn't do so well. I remember getting up to go to the bathroom;

my urine in the water was brown. Dang, I thought! I have to make a much more considerable effort to drink more water. So, I videoed my sister, we talked, and she said she would call me throughout the day to make sure I was drinking better. Unbeknownst to me, she took a screenshot of me each time we talked. I have seen one picture, and it is well documented that I was pretty sick. I spent the next few days in bed, only making limited trips to the bathroom and asking my son for more popsicles. He was able to stay home from work and take care of me, and I am forever thankful. For those curious, our kids never got sick from being around me. Our dog would wander in and look at me with a sad dog face. He was worried. He knew momma was ill.

But then Saturday came. I felt different. Not great, but there was a change. I decided to take a shower, and I didn't faint. That was a win. The following executive decision was to move out to the couch for the day. And that was also a win. I continued to sleep a lot and was definitely in bed by 8 pm…if I made it that late. I would frequently fall asleep as my husband and I FaceTimed each night. The exhaustion that came with COVID was no joke. And the recovery for me was at a glacial pace.

HOW WE WERE ADVOCATES FOR OUR MARRIAGE

That week I made another decision. I had to go on short-term disability. There was absolutely no way that I could work, recover from COVID, and finish my chemotherapy treatment. I knew I had to give my body a break, which was through short-term disability. My Nurse Practitioner agreed and wrote the order for me to not work until after my chemotherapy treatment was complete. The combo of COVID and chemo kicked me down completely. And I was beyond thankful for this allowance in our benefits coverage. My sage advice for anyone who gets a cancer diagnosis with chemotherapy is just to start your short-term disability immediately if you absolutely can. I understand it is a percentage of your pay, but your body will thank you profusely. And the long-term benefit of tolerating this treatment and giving your body the best fighting chance is non-negotiable.

From mid-August until the beginning of November, I spent the days on my couch in our living room or on the lanai during the day. I would either be upright or horizontal. My body slowly regained strength; but until chemotherapy had ended, I had no commitments except eating, sleeping, and short walks in our cul-de-sac to let our dog do his job.

Qualified Advocates

The first day I started my treatment, my chemotherapy lead nurse shared something that changed my mindset. Nurse, Julie, looked at me lovingly and said, "We are not the family you want to belong to. But if you have to be part of this family, we are the ones you want to be part of." She understood that each patient she initiated care with was scared. She looked at each of us and made us feel seen and understood. I immediately trusted her and her team. Each one of the infusion team had a huge heart and made sure you knew that you were important to them. I knew they had my back from the first day of treatment. I knew they would be my advocate every step, and they were. Not a treatment week went by that made me unsure of the next step or what to do when I had a question. I was well educated and loved every step of the way. That is an excellent example of an advocate. Everyone needs a "Julie" in their corner in an uncertain situation.

My Family—The A Team

Why are we the "A" team? Pretty simple—Art, Ann, Alex, Amelia, and Aaron. And, of course, Andy, the dog. And to say that they delivered on being the A+ Team through my cancer diagnosis is not to be minimized.

My husband, Art, is the understated hero in our lives. Like my father, he is a man of few words. But he is our everything. He is our solid rock and the firm foundation in our family. He just does. He has always been the provider in our family. He has coached our boys' sports teams. He has fixed everything in our homes. He has that mechanical knowledge that is valued from my point of view.

On the spiritual side, our daughter said it best about her dad. "Mom, you always ensured we went to church every Sunday. But when you worked your weekends at the hospital and Dad made sure we were in church and Sunday School on those days, I knew our faith life was significant." Moments like this make a momma cry happy tears. Our kids need a father present in all areas of their lives; and spiritually, they need a dad who shares and passes his faith onto them until they make it their own.

Art's living in Vermont and Wisconsin during this time of my health challenges was taxing on him. He felt like he was not here for me. Physically, he was right. But emotionally, he was all in; and I felt his presence 24/7. I was so appreciative of texting. Because I could text him at any time to let him know of any changes or needs, and he could answer them during his work day as he had time. And we were so thankful for FaceTime. We used it daily and for an obnoxious amount of time. We sometimes just watched our favorite shows together while we were FaceTiming. Sometimes it is just the knowledge that we were "together" that melted the miles between us.

He was able to travel enough during this time to make it bearable for both of us. We were so thankful for his leaders at both companies, who had immeasurable amounts of grace to let him travel to see me when it was most important. Art has always been a great leader for his teams, so even when he was with me, he was always available via phone for his teams. He never left them alone. One of his many marks of excellence—He loves his team members, and his team feels it immediately when they first meet him.

And God answered a prayer that we started praying the day I put him on the plane on January 30, 2020. The prayer to return him home at the perfect timing. And he answered that prayer late one night in February of 2022 when his boss, Mark, from Florida, called and asked Art if he wanted his job back in Florida! Art about dropped his phone and said yes before Mark could say anything more.

It was after all of my health challenges were healed, and we were so thankful as we drove home from Wisconsin in March of 2022 TOGETHER! Our family from across the nation was happy, and our neighbors threw up a few loud shouts of thanksgiving, too! We all missed Art on the street.

He jokingly says, after 30 years of marriage, "We are always on the same path; you are just a few steps ahead of me." And he is right. I am the idea girl in our relationship, but the ideas I dream up are to make our lives more joyful and full of sparkle. And Art makes all of my thoughts a reality. And our life is beautiful because of his love for me.

Art has been my advocate since the day we met. Not all advocates are the same. Some are the steady current in your life and the ones who keep you afloat when you feel as though you are going to go down and drown. And that's who Art is. He is my steady. Everyone needs an Art in their life.

Our kids played a role as I went through this journey. We commended them along the way, as this event brought out each of their talents front and center. They stepped up when I had to lie down. They did more than was asked without even being asked. Our neighbors have continuously reaffirmed what each parent's goal is when they start raising their kids. They and many people we know always say, "You have the nicest kids." We agree wholeheartedly. We are not perfect parents, and each child can attest to a few shortcomings that we each have; but together we have worked to raise them to love God, respect others, and have a good work ethic. And I think we have done a pretty good job and will continue to parent them until the end.

Everyone needs an Alex, Amelia, and Aaron in their life. The work of Godly parenting pays off in making this world a better place by "raising the next generation of Christian leaders." Thank you, Mayer Lutheran High, for not only sharing this quote but for living it out by being the educators who played an essential role in raising our children to be the next generation of Christian leaders at your school for four years of their education.

Qualities of an Advocate

As a nurse, I have always enjoyed the people who visit our patients. Only a slim minority of visitors in labor and delivery were not helpful. The visitors who were there for "the show" of the baby's birth are not beneficial for the patient. I alluded to this above, but valuable visitors are there to support the patient, ask questions for the patient, which help us clarify the care plan for the patient, and speak up if the patient is unable to. High-quality visitors genuinely make the patient experience better. Many patients were not afforded this option during the height of COVID, and the care of many patients suffered.

I want to speak in the general sense of adding value to your journey or someone you know about advocacy. We need and can be advocates for anyone in a variety of situations. There are also many things we can do to be an advocate. There are also many ways not to be an effective advocate. Let's discuss a few of the beneficial ways of being an advocate.

As the Bible talks about advocates, John explains how Jesus shares with His disciples that God will be sending an advocate through the Holy Spirit. Because Jesus knew He would not be with the disciples for very long, there would be a new "person." It is explained in John 14:14-21. As believers, we know we have the gift of the Holy Spirit within us, and we can feel his presence throughout our lives. He guides us in making decisions, adding to our wisdom and countless other things we take for granted. But the Holy Spirit is there.

Another spot in the Bible that points out an advocate is the Parable of the Good Samaritan, in Luke 10:25-37. In this story, the most unlikely person became the advocate for the most despised. I understand that so much as a nurse. Even though I think our hospital gowns are the most hideous thing ever seen, they put everyone on an equal playing field. When I meet a patient lying in a bed, I have no worldly indication of who they are. I know the facts of their medical history and what has brought them into my care. And this was brought so clearly to my attention one fateful day when I was serving a meal to the homeless and people in need in a city we lived near. I locked eyes with a young gal who had young children with her. I KNEW HER. I knew her in a patient gown. I remembered her time under my care as soon as I saw her. I had no clue during her care what her real life was like outside of the hospital. But that day made me remember how important my role was as a nurse to give superior care to all of my patients. It didn't matter what their bags looked like or how their visitors were dressed. Every mom that I cared for received the best from me.

We had a privilege as we worked in labor and delivery that is not seen in the other parts of the hospital. We take care of patients in some very vulnerable moments. I was trained throughout my career by many physicians and nurses. They all had great ways to help our moms stay calm during pretty hectic and unexpected birth experiences. And I took cues from each of them and added their expertise to my "bag of tricks" to deliver excellent care.

One of the skills we learn as L/D nurses is how to deliver a baby. It turns out that no matter how close our doctors are on the unit or in the hospital, sometimes those babies arrive before they can run down the halls and put their gloves on. I will never forget the day Dr. Strathy looked at me when I called her into the room with time to spare to deliver this baby. She smiled and said, "Sit down on that bed and deliver this baby." I had been a nurse for quite a while, but the doctors always surprised us with the opportunity to deliver a baby under their careful surveillance. And so I delivered that baby with Dr. Strathy right by my side. It's a rush of adrenaline that I miss. And as I type this, I miss Dr. Strathy, too. She was with me on the most challenging day in my nursing career, and the next day as she saw me enter the nurse's station, she quietly handed me a note as she attended to a patient. I opened it and read these words: "You have my utmost respect." I had to keep my composure among my coworkers, but I kept that note for a long time. It spoke life into me the rest of my time on that unit.

Everyone needs some great doctors in their lives to learn from, and I had many at the different hospitals where I worked in the Midwest. Thank you to each and every one of you who impacted the level of care I provided as a nurse.

To be an effective advocate for yourself or a loved one at any point, you want to remember a few basics. Always start with facts. Know the history of the patient/person you advocate for during your care. Ask questions for clarification and to expand the level of information that you are trying to get from the medical team/leadership. A few other things that are good to do is to take notes to refer to later, ask for the research/references the team is referencing, and always know it is ok to ask for another opinion. The last critical basic of being an effective advocate is to remain respectful. I have always shared that I believe the reason I was so impressed with my care team is that they knew I was curious and just wanted to know more information. They knew I was searching for complete understanding so that I would be comfortable with each step of my treatment, and they respected me for my curiosity. I was respectful with all of my questions and inquiries.

Lastly, I want to share that you do not have to have a nursing or medical degree to be a good advocate in a medical situation. Ask more questions than you usually feel comfortable doing. It is ok to ask "why?" one more time. The more you ask why, the more likely you will get an honest answer with a more detailed explanation. You and your loved ones deserve excellent care. I and others in the medical field love to educate. We always want to ensure that you know what we are doing and why we are doing it. That is the basis of informed consent. Please see the list of "high quality questions" at the end of this chapter for you to use at any time during your health journey.

As with most things in life, we are sometimes called to be an advocate without much advance notice. That's where being intentional with your relationships with certain people is critical to this piece. It is essential to ask your family members about their medical history or other pertinent details that may help you in any circumstance. This is why building deep, trusted relationships with those surrounding you is essential. You may be called to do more than you can imagine right now. The intention in our living means being an advocate for ourselves always and for others when we are called upon.

Questions to Journal

How have I prepared to be an advocate?

If not, what ideas were stirred as you read this chapter?

Have I been allowed to be an advocate and not followed through?

What will I do differently going forward if given another opportunity to be an advocate when I feel unprepared or caught by surprise? What is the next right thing you need to do/learn to prepare for the role of advocate?

_____

_____

_____

_____

_____

_____

_____

_____

_____

_____

_____

_____

High Quality Questions

1. Come to the doctor with a list of questions.

2. Bring someone along with you—four ears are better than two.

3. If you don't understand the answers provided, ask for plainer language.

4. Don't be afraid to say you don't understand and always rephrase the answer back to the doctor to see if you are correct.

5. Needing further clarification: How can you help me find out the answer to those questions?

6. How can you help me do that? Will you talk with your colleagues and help me find more information?

7. Can you do some research or ask about some referrals?

8. If you are not likely to follow the advice, ask for help in how to make the changes.

9. If lifestyle modifications are required, ask which would be the one thing that would be most important. (little steps)

10. Don't be afraid to tell your physician that you haven't been able to do what you were asked to do—exercise, take medication, eat differently etc—as you don't want to be put on another medication when you haven't been taking/doing the first.

11. Who is the "expert" in the local/regional area for X condition/stage of life/illness?

12. What is the failure rate of this surgery or procedure? (There are always risks and side effects to all procedures/surgeries.)

13. What are other options or things that I can do to help with that? I want to feel as normal as possible. Describe your normal routine.

14. Are your discharge instructions clear so I will have them to reference at home?
    a. What are normal signs of healing after my surgery?
    b. How will my GI system function—for example—as it heals?
    c. What are good foods to eat after my procedure to promote healing?
    d. What foods should I stay away from right after or during the recovery stage?
    e. Can you describe the activity level I should start at and then progress to from discharge through the first 6 weeks of recovery?

The following are from Time [1]

1. Do we have to do this now, or can we revisit it later?
2. Is there anything I can do on my own to improve my condition?
3. What questions haven't I asked that I should have?

The following are from Cleveland Clinic [2]

1. What caused the disease or condition?
2. Is there any further testing I will need?
3. What are my treatment options? Risks/benefits, length, what would happen if I delay treatment?
4. What is the short-term and long-term prognosis?

The following are from USNews [3]

1. How does my family history affect my risk for certain health conditions?
2. How could my condition/diagnosis affect my health down the road?
3. What do you do for your personal wellness?
4. My real fear is X—how concerned should I be?

Questions specific for oncology can be found from Square One Healing Cancer Coaching Program. [4]

CHAPTER 7

INTENTION—PRAYER

THE DOXOLOGY

Praise God from whom all blessings flow,

Praise Him all creatures here below,

Praise Him above ye heavenly hosts,

Praise Father, Son, and Holy Ghost. Amen. [1]

Conversations. After waking up from my colonoscopy, I started having many discussions and understood I had a problem. I had a lot to process and a lot to learn. As I have shared, I reached out to my friends in the medical field and started asking questions to learn more information. Sometimes, I wasn't even sure what to ask for during each conversation. I wanted to know all the good, bad, and ugly data. I was praying for hope in each conversation.

I reached out to those with faith like mine. They shared Scriptures that comforted them and reminded me to pray for God's will to be done. Those five words are the hardest to pray for as that is the reminder that God's will is perfect and also reminds us that we are not in control of our lives or health. God has the final say.

One of my favorite ways to pray is to pray through songs. There are an unlimited number of hymns and worship songs that are a great way to pray our deepest prayers through their lyrics. I was raised as a Lutheran, and our hymns were rooted in God's Word; and the melody that came with them helped those verses become part of our permanent memory. I have cousins who have become accomplished organists. And when I am privileged enough to sit in the pews as they play on a Sunday morning, the tears just roll. They are happy tears as I reflect upon the meaning of what I am singing as their God-given gifts come alive through the sound that comes from those organs. Rhonda, Lois, and Denise have been given these gifts through their fingers and feet, and God's glory shines bright each time they slide onto the bench and turn on their respective organs.

I don't live near my cousins anymore, so I rely heavily on YouTube to listen to worship songs. I have created a playlist to listen to daily and pray through their music. Use these as a springboard to creating your own playlist for daily prayer through song if that resonates with you.

- "El Shaddai" and "Thy Word Mix" by Amy Grant
- "Raise a Hallelujah" (Live) by Bethel Music (I love to hear the story behind the song)
- "Way Maker" by Paul McClure
- "10,000 Reasons" by Matt Redman
- "Graves into Gardens" by Elevation Worship
- "Who You Say I Am" by Hillsong Worship
- "Our God" by Chris Tomlin
- "Tell Your Heart to Beat Again" (Live) by Danny Gokey (he shares the story behind the song)
- "How Great Thou Art" by Carrie Underwood featuring Vince Gill

As I repeatedly listened to the song "Raise a Hallelujah," it became my anthem as I fought alongside God to heal my body. As they created this, they prayed to see the miracle of healing for this little boy, Jackson. And one night, they received the news that he might not make it through the night and their thoughts were, "We are not going to see the miracle." (from the intro of this song on YouTube) [2]

Many times I listened to this testimony and how this song was brought to creation; and as I listened to that quote, "they were not going to see the miracle," I thought to myself, this was not complete. The thought that came to me when we pray, we generally pray for earthly healing. We want whoever we are praying for to be healed and to continue their life here on earth. We have this sense that life on earth is "the best." We don't want to lose them. BUT, God revealed to me something that gives me more comfort as I pray, "God's Will be done." Sometimes He answers prayer and does let us see the miraculous healing here on earth. But, there are times that the miracle of healing occurs through death. For believers in Jesus, the ultimate miracle is the healing when we experience an earthly death and run into our Savior's arms with our perfect heavenly bodies because of His death and resurrection.

I will never forget the day I was at my GI doctor following up after my colonoscopy. The med techs were doing my vitals, and we were having a lively conversation that turned quickly to God. They knew my likely diagnosis. And I looked at them and exclaimed, "Whatever the outcome, Jesus has conquered my cancer diagnosis at the cross." That I was sure of, and they readily agreed with me. I had to walk through the "mess" of surgery, diagnosis, and treatment. BUT I could walk confidently, KNOWING that Jesus had won the battle. And from that day, I pivoted. I walked with a "Holy Swagger," as Christians sometimes say.

Walk with Godfidence, because He WILL give us everything to rise up and serve.

I still had moments of doubt and fear that would creep in, but overall I focused on Jesus' triumphant victory that Easter Sunday morning many years ago.

After my surgery, one of my conversations turned to a specific prayer request. I asked Susie to pray alongside me as I asked God to keep my "pendulum" of emotions steady. I had experienced so many emotional highs and lows, and I knew it was not suitable for any part of my body or healing. So we prayed that God would steady my emotions. And He answered that prayer. I slowly and steadily saw that I was experiencing His comfort, and my feelings were becoming more steady. It is incredible to see God heal all parts of your body. It is particularly mind-blowing to see Him heal your mindset and your emotions. We all have a "common enemy" in our mind as it can spiral downward at the flip of a switch. I will go more in-depth about our mindset later.

In Fall 2012, I started reading the book, "The Circle Maker" by Mark Batterson. He referenced the Jewish collection of stories from the Talmud and Midrash, The Book of Legends, which contains the teachings of Jewish rabbis passed down from generation to generation. It was the legend of Honi on page 19, the circle maker. And it forever changed the way Mark prayed. [3] I learned many things to incorporate in different times as I prayed in the future.

I encourage you to read the book. I didn't physically change the way I prayed right away. I didn't have anything I thought I needed to pray around, but I kept this idea in my mind until I saw what I specifically had to "circle" in prayer.

Fast forward to my diagnosis and the journey that followed. My prayer life moved from the customary and specific prayers for our family, friends, etc., to a level I had never experienced. My prayers became real intimate with God. I talked with God on a 24/7 basis. Sometimes it was in a regular cadence, and it progressed to some loud sobs as I was crying uncontrollably. Thank goodness God can understand our prayers that arrive in heaven in all languages and sometimes as tears.

At this time, I had gathered my prayer team. The prayers of my prayer team were being raised in a steady stream. I was humbled and beyond thankful that I had people from all over to pray for my family and me, my healthcare team, and pray that God's will would be done. We saw many prayers answered in a steady cadence. It is always incredible to see how God works.

My prayers continued as I got through the most complex parts of my journey. They changed and took on a different focus. But God kept prompting me to pray for my surgeon, the anesthesia team, my pre-op nurse, and my oncology team, which I affectionately roll into "My Favorite Hospital." God kept prompting me every morning as I walked with Andy to lift them in prayer. I wondered why? My thought was that I was "done" with that part of my chapter. God reminded me that they needed prayer every day. They were now someone's healthcare team, and each patient needed prayer, as I did on March 22, 2021. God taught me to pray for all, including those I don't personally know. It has been a powerful lesson, and I am humbled to be the daily "anonymous" prayer warrior for each patient and every member of "My Favorite Hospital."

As I regained my strength, endurance, and pace, I remembered the book, "Circle Maker." And I thought I could "circle" "My Favorite Hospital" in prayer. I don't live that far away. Andy likes to go for a car ride and is game for walking in new neighborhoods. So, we started a new routine. On Friday or Saturday, we jump in the car, drive to the hospital and walk around the facility and the nearby neighborhoods. My prayer starts for this team and branches outward from there. God brings to my mind those who need prayer, and I add those specific prayers daily.

I don't know what this team needs daily, but I pray for them. My prayer goes something like this each morning:

Dear God. I lift up Dr. E, Dr. G, Dr. B, Dr. K, Maribel, and all of those working in the Pre-Op/OR/PACU today. Please be present in each of the ORs and guide each surgeon's hands. Provide great wisdom to the anesthesia team as they put everyone to sleep and wake each of them up. Give comfort to each patient as they are under their care. May those unaware of you have their hearts softened at your specific timing. Please be with the workers and leadership at "My Favorite Hospital." I also pray for their families as they give up so much of their loved ones' time when they are called in to care for patients in need. You know their specific prayer requests, and I lift them up to you now. May each of them come to know you. In Jesus' name, I pray. Amen.

Prayers from Generation to Generation

My sister shared something she learned as she spent a few weeks with our parents early in 2022. Our dad farmed and spent many hours planting, cultivating, and harvesting in the fields. He started in the 1960s and farmed until the fall of 2010. The only thing he had in a few of his tractors was a rough excuse for a radio. During those hours driving up and down the rows of his fields, I never thought of what he thought. And when my sister shared that, he prayed. I was in awe, not surprised, but genuinely thankful.

Our dad prayed. He prayed for hours, most likely. He prayed day in and day out on his John Deere tractors. As I have shared, our dad was a man of few words. He loved Jesus, and it showed in so many ways. He didn't have to talk about His relationship with Jesus for us to know how close he was to our Lord and Savior.

When you farm, you are entirely at the mercy of the weather, the markets who set the prices for the seed, the harvest, and the price he was quoted when he would sell the cattle and the pigs. Farmers are not in control of any of their pricing. Our dad never seemed on edge. There was a peace about him that I marveled at as he farmed through the years. And as my emotions swung wildly during my initial diagnosis, I always remembered how calm our dad was.

Our dad knowing this information, knew he was completely within God's mercy. He knew God would protect him and our family. He knew that God would bless his harvest each year. He knew that God would see our family through the good and lean years. He knew this because our dad prayed. Our dad was also in the church pew every Sunday; even during planting and harvest season, he never missed church. He knew that God would honor his faithfulness of church attendance even in the midst of planting and harvest seasons. That's how much faith he had in Jesus. He never worried openly because He took everything to Jesus in prayer as he worked. He also participated in the men's Bible studies at our church. He was also on the boards and leadership teams of our church. Our dad modeled so many things with his faith.

I have seen my dad cry three times so far. He wasn't emotionless. He loved us, and we knew it. He involved us in all parts of his love of farming. We had a blessed life in that manner. But he showed his emotions when it was due. His mom died when I was 16. Not only did our dad cry. We all did. The last hymn of her funeral was "I Know that My Redeemer Lives" and there was not a dry eye in the church as we all sung together in the midst of our tears. I still cry anytime we sing that hymn. Then there was a late spring blizzard one year. My dad bred the cows so they would calve in April, after the winter storms have subsided in Iowa. But one year, God sent a blizzard after some calves had been born and the calves and their moms had been put back out in the field. In the 1980s, we didn't have the weather channel app on our smartphones. We had phones attached to the wall; the only weather forecast came at 6 am, noon, 6 pm, and the 10 pm news broadcasts. The storm was not well predicted, and my dad lost some new calves as they froze to death. My dad cried. We all sobbed that morning. The other time I saw my dad cry was when our oldest son left for Bootcamp to serve in the Marine Corps. We all sobbed along with him. My dad and our oldest son had formed a bond like no other after a summer spent together before our son entered high school. Their relationship ran deep, and his commitment to serve our country struck a chord in my dad's heart that brought him to tears the last time he saw him before the send-off. But now, each Memorial Day, my dad proudly sports the Marine Corps tie my mom found him to wear in honor of Alex's service. I cry each year as I see him tie that tie around his neck before he goes to church on the last Sunday of May.

Not only did my dad pray, but my parents prayed together each morning and before they went to bed. They modeled to all of us that our days should start and end with God. My parents were fervent prayer warriors all of our lives. And we knew that when it looked turbulent in our lives, they were praying specifically for us and that God's will would be done. You never outgrow the need for your parents' prayers.

As you look at the book cover, the picture behind the words was photographed by my brother, Rick. It is a picture of my dad combining his last field of beans. It's the inspiration for the book title and what I am writing. My dad prayed all those days in the fields as he worked. He was sowing seeds of our faith in his prayers along with sowing corn and soybeans. I don't think he prayed that I would grow up and become an author. But I do believe he prayed that each of us would have a strong faith in Jesus and that we would lean into the God-given gifts Jesus bestowed onto us. He prayed for our generation and each generation that follows. That blows my mind. But the knowledge of those prayers he prayed has profoundly impacted me, especially as a parent. He "planted" seeds in each of us to sow for our children and the generations that follow them. Our dad prayed the prayers that covered every aspect of our lives, marriages, careers, and all the details he couldn't even express. And Jesus heard them. And Jesus will continue to answer these prayers for generations to come. Our dad not only sowed seeds of field corn and soybeans; he sowed seeds of faith for generations to come. And we are now continuing praying for the next generations just as our parents showed us.

Prayers From Those You Don't Know

Because our family lives in different states of this great nation, we attend different churches. If you are familiar with churches, you know that you can submit prayer requests, and the Pastors and their prayer circles will pray for you. I had many churches praying for me. These members were praying to God on my behalf. As Christians, we say we were storming heaven with prayers for Ann. I knew my home church was praying as they knew me from birth. But, my sister's church, Lord of Glory, in Grayslake, IL, didn't physically know me. They knew my sister because their family is involved in that church. My sister added my specific prayers each week, and they prayed. They have a therapy dog, Tobias, so the dog was involved too. In addition to the prayers, I started receiving a card from their prayer team monthly that Miss Sandy lovingly wrote and sent. All the details touched me as different people included them in their prayers. After I finished my treatment, I was able to travel to Chicagoland for a family event and was able to stay for church one Sunday. I sat down in church, and people recognized me as I sat by my sister. After church was finished, it was like a welcome event. I met everyone. I cried with them as I thanked them for all of the prayers they had said. I hugged Tobias. I thanked his trainer for all of her prayers. It is incredible to wrap your head around the unselfish love that we receive from others through prayer.

There is something incredible about the Christian community. We pray. We pray for those we know and their prayer requests. We also pray for those we don't know. So most likely, someone is praying for you right now. Even if you haven't asked or don't even know God, it's safe to say that you are covered in prayer by the prayer warriors of the world.

Here are a few notes on praying that I have learned throughout my life and would like to share with you now. Jesus gave us the order to pray as He taught us the Lord's Prayer in Matthew 6:9-13. Jesus also prays a prayer in the chapter of John 17, which is a great one to pray. I have learned from a BSF teaching leader, Candace, that we can insert names of those we know in this passage as Jesus says "they." That is a great way to personalize this specific Scripture when praying. I have also learned that we can open up the Bible and pray any Scripture; specifically, Psalms are good to use as prayers. I hope these suggestions are helpful and inspire other ideas for you in this area. There are many ideas, acronyms, and many books written about praying. Don't overthink praying. Just talk to God.

Talking with God should resemble conversations that you have with your closest friend.

I want to close this chapter with a prayer shared on Mother's Day by our Pastor's wife, Danita.

(Permission granted by K Parker.)

> *Father, through your power and under your authority,*
> *I will lead. I expect to be:*
> *A source of truth to those in deception,*
> *A source of hope for those in despair.*
> *A source of faith for those in doubt.*
> *A source of peace for those who are anxious.*
> *A source of forgiveness for those who are bitter.*
> *A source of love for those who feel despised.*
> *In the name of Jesus, Amen.* [4]

Go lead!

Questions to Journal

Am I content with my prayer life, or are there some areas that I want to add in?

What new ideas for your prayer life were brought to light as you read this chapter?

How has this prompted me to be more purposeful in praying for unexpected things in our world—local to global?

_____

_____

_____

_____

_____

_____

_____

_____

_____

_____

_____

_____

_____

_____

_____

CHAPTER 8

INTENTION—PRIORITIES AND PURPOSE

"Be strong and very courageous. Be careful to obey all the law my servant Moses gave you; do not turn from it to the right or to the left, that you may be successful wherever you go. Do not let this book of the Law depart from your mouth; meditate on it day and night, so that you may be careful to do everything written in it. You will be prosperous and successful."

JOSHUA 1:7-8 NIV

We all have an order of priorities in our lives. Some people have a very well-thought-out order of their importance, and others have a vague concept of the idea. And, of course, there are many people somewhere in the middle of this concept. Oxford language defines intention as an aim or plan. Knowing your priorities from most important to least important further clarifies having an aim or a plan and keeps the focus on intention in our lives.

I have felt that I have had a pretty good grasp on my priorities, especially as I zeroed in on the importance of health. And that is what I want to focus on in this chapter. I will cover the broader order of priorities in a later chapter.

Grandpa Berry's Story

I learned early in my life the value of health. I was in Junior High in the early 1980s when my Grandpa's health abruptly changed. He had known he had a defective aortic valve in his heart. For those of you who need a refresh on the anatomy of your heart—your aorta is the major artery that takes freshly oxygenated blood from your heart to your entire body. It generally has three flaps; my Grandpa's had two. The two flaps had worked well for most of his life.

But one fall afternoon in the middle of his golf game, he experienced a heart attack as he was putting. His buddies started CPR and somehow got someone else's attention to call 9-1-1. They revived him, bringing him to the local hospital to be stabilized. Our cousin, Trudy, ended up being his RN in the ICU at this hospital. Her expertise in critical care put our family at ease until the medical staff could implement a better plan for transfer. He needed a new heart valve, and his doctors were able to secure a referral to a tertiary hospital in Omaha, Nebraska.

He was transferred and had a successful new metal heart valve placed. This opportunity to observe what happens after cardiac surgery and through the recovery phase positively impacted me and continued to stoke the idea of me being a nurse. I loved seeing how they were all taking care of my Grandpa. As my Grandpa neared his time for discharge, the cardiac surgeon gave him some pretty detailed instructions that my Grandpa thoroughly listened to and ended up changing his lifestyle. Following his discharge instructions is precisely what his surgeon wanted him to do with this new heart valve.

What were his instructions? Walk every day for an hour, no excuses. Eat lots of veggies every day and minimize your red meat consumption. Three things.

Simple. BUT…the question was—Was my Grandpa going to commit to it? Oh yes! And he followed the instructions each day of his life until shortly before his death at ninety-one years old. Three simple instructions and he followed them to the letter. He did have two knees replaced simultaneously, and broke two other bones in the meantime. In the end, his orthopedic doctor was also happy to have my Grandpa as a patient!

Let's talk this through. I firmly believe that God has our days numbered. I also know that we are given free will to make all the choices during our life. I believe that our health and the outcomes are a mixture of these two factors, God's will and our choices. Let me state this another way, if you look at a set of twins who make the exact same choices throughout their lives, I can guarantee they will have different medical diagnosis and different outcomes. Maybe not significantly different, but they will not be exactly the same. With this clarification, let's get back to the wisdom imparted by that cardiac surgeon in the mid-1980s when health/wellness was on a slim number of people's minds.

This surgeon instructed my Grandpa to walk for an hour every day. My Grandpa made a plan and kept to it. He lived a block away from his Catholic parish, which had a school gym. After sharing the instructions from his surgeon, he asked the Priest if he could walk there each day. The Priest readily agreed. My Grandpa also asked his best friend to join him. Two points are evident here. He had a spot to walk in all seasons of Iowa weather and a friend to keep him accountable. He overcame two common obstacles that stop almost everyone from being consistent with their activity. He made it easy and enjoyable.

When the surgeon gave the instructions to my Grandpa to eat more veggies and decrease red meat, I think my Grandma ran over and hugged him with the biggest hug that had ever been given. She was far ahead of everyone in the healthy eating subject. My mom still shares that my Grandma never made Jell-O or kool-aid when my mom was growing up. So, this instruction was quickly carried out as my Grandma was a very healthy cook. Done and dusted. My Grandpa had one vacation meal every week. They joined us for lunch after church each Sunday, and he had beef nachos. He followed the instructions to the exact syllable.

How About Me?

I grew up eating "farm food." My dad raised Black Angus cattle and pigs to sell, and the meat would end up in your local grocery store. He would have one of each butchered each year, and we had two large chest freezers that we would "shop" from each day for our meals. My mom planted a large garden in our backyard, which she tended well each year; and we harvested as the vegetables became ripe each summer. Any added bounty would be frozen or canned. My dad also planted a few rows of sweet corn in his field for us to eat fresh and then freeze the excess. We were blessed to know our farmer, and the food we ate was fresh from the garden. My mom did shop at the grocery store for a few things; our grocery store was tiny. It was the size of a corner store. The same grocery chain has outgrown this original place twice and is quite large because of all the processed foods that are now readily sold in grocery stores across our country.

I learned as I grew up the fine art of canning and freezing. I also was taught how to cook and bake everything "from scratch." I spent many hours in our kitchen with my mom. I still love to cook and bake. I have left my canning and freezing skills on the farm as I didn't make planting and tending a garden a priority in my adult life. When I married my husband, I was elated to be a "city" girl. I couldn't wait to have a large grocery store near and not have to work as hard in the kitchen. I embraced a lot of processed foods in my cooking. I had a stash of Campbell's soups, Pillsbury crescent rolls, and frozen items to fill out our kitchen inventory. My husband has always been in the baking industry, so we have had a steady supply of bagels, garlic bread, and pizza. To say we have eaten the "Standard American Diet" (SAD) in our marriage is an understatement. And we didn't pay the price of this right away, and nor do most people. The Starbucks' iced hazelnut latte doesn't go right to your hip. And the four or five pieces of

Art's garlic bread don't immediately go to your waistline either. We may have been bloated after most meals, though.

But, we did feel and see the effects of the Standard American Diet, eventually. We were sick at the appropriate cycles, carried more weight on our bodies than we should have, bloated, etc. But it all tasted so good. Red meat is not all that bad, right? Those "crunchy" people can't be right about it, can they? Take out gluten? Are you serious? My husband is a B-A-K-E-R. You have tasted all those yummy things he makes, right?? How can we make those changes? We have always eaten that way and so far we aren't "sick."

I Started a Business

And then, something happened in 2006. I was introduced to a wellness company that produces nutrition and skincare products with extremely high development and protection standards. And I started to learn. I was at every conference, at all the meetings, read every book recommended, and used all the products. A few years later, I participated in a 30-day "Detox" eating plan. At that time, elimination plans were new; and most people were hesitant. No gluten, no dairy, no sugar, no processed foods were key items to remove for the timeframe. It included real food and our company's nutrition products. We affectionately called it the "Twigs and Berries Diet." I called my friend on the first day at 2 pm and said, "I. AM. STARVING!" She reminded me that we had been provided recipes and we would follow this all the way. Ok, she talked me off the ledge, and I recommitted to doing the plan.

And then I went to work at the hospital the next day. Of course, I shared with some of my coworkers what I was doing; and I felt they were putting me under a microscope while I was at work. And, of course, a few hours after I arrived, one of the doctors on-call came strolling through the nurse's station with a layered chocolate cake because it was her birthday. I almost screamed. But then all the eyes of my coworkers fell in my direction. They were dying to see if I would cave on day two. And I was like, nope. You all just gave me an additional dose of resolve. I was going to follow this plan and not waiver ONCE. I politely told the doctor no thank you, drank a glass of water, and went in to take care of my patient.

How did it go? It was a learning experience. We had a short list of recipes that fit all the qualifications, so that was a little challenging, but I made it. I did feel better. My skin was clear. And I was pretty excited to pull on the scrubs with the yellow ties (small) at my waist instead of the brown ties (medium.) I was in the small-size of scrubs now!! It worked. Many of my co-workers were shocked, but they couldn't disagree with the results. Take out all the allergenic foods and the sugar, and your body is ecstatic. I like to equate it with changing your furnace filter routinely. Amazing how well our body works when we treat it well. You can lose weight if you need to. Your body will return to homeostasis if we give it the chance with healthy choices.

I had been an avid learner before this "30-day Detox," and this lit a passion in me that was next level. I had experienced it. I wanted more information. I wanted to know this information on a deeper level. This company was on the right path. Whole foods, remove the most likely allergenic foods, drink water, eat only from 7 am–7 pm, exercise, sleep well and utilize their nutrition products. It wasn't a way-out-there concept. But it seemed like it, given the "standard American diet." We are so used to eating non-food that when we switch back to whole foods or real food that doesn't have an ingredient list on it, people think we have joined a cult.

I continued my learning. I started revamping our family's nutrition plan, which I will share more in-depth later. I took the next step in my commitment. My mindset had changed because I experienced the shift, and the knowledge I was acquiring cemented the fact I was on the right track. I was going back to the basics honestly, and everyone thought I had lost my mind.

The Swine Flu Episode

But then my husband got sick. Do you remember the Swine Flu? I do, vividly. My husband has a variety of respiratory allergies and breathing problems which were exasperated with this diagnosis. I had earned a trip to Mexico with my company and was in my hotel room briefly when the phone rang. It was my husband. And I thought, this is not good; he sounded bad. He had just left Urgent Care. They assessed him, gave him a breathing treatment, and x-rays, and told him that he might have flour-induced emphysema. Holy crap! All of these details are not good, and I was at a resort in Mexico. He said he would be fine until I arrived home on Saturday. I hung up the phone and prayed.

Our kids were old enough to take care of themselves while their dad was ill. Luckily, it was a long weekend for Minnesota schools, so they all stayed home. Art passed out, and the kids hung out and made do for meals. I arrived home on Saturday afternoon, pushed my suitcase in, and ran to our bedroom. And I assessed him. The quick head-to-toe assessment was not encouraging. I loaded him into the car, and we were on the way back to the Urgent Care. They did a few more breathing treatments and new antibiotics. I was mad about the fragmented care, but knew I could take care of him until I could get him to our PCP on Monday morning.

Monday morning came, and I made an appointment asap. Our doctor looked at him after I gave him a brief report, and said, "He has the swine flu. I should admit him, but he will likely get sicker in the hospital." He looked at me and said, "I am sending him home with you." He gave me the parameters to watch for; and if he met these, I was to bring him into the ER. He gave us more specific antibiotics and a tapering dose of Prednisone. It's the fringe benefit of your PCP knowing your skills as a nurse. So, I walked him to the car, and halfway out he almost fainted. I was thinking, this is not really going well. The next few hours were touch and go, but he made it through the roughest part. The Prednisone made him very sleepy. He slept for twenty hours each day for the next ten days.

I moved into our daughter's room to sleep, and we cleaned the bathroom with Clorox after each time he used it. He drank two protein shakes daily and slept the rest of the time.

He recovered, and the next step was to have him seen by a cardio-thoracic doctor a friend highly recommended. I wanted a close look at his lungs after the Urgent Care doctor had suggested a type of emphysema from working around flour for years. Art had developed an enlarged heart during this recent illness. Thankfully, with the recheck, his heart returned to standard size. The doctor was blown away, and we gave all the credit to God. And after further evaluation, there was no diagnosis of emphysema. Another praise!

My Quest Continued

After that experience, my resolve continued to deepen. We, as a family, needed to completely pivot in the nutrition realm and commit with a goal being as close to one hundred percent as we could attain. I was going to do as much as possible to add health to our family. We were going to make changes that would give our bodies the best opportunity to be vital to hopefully keep disease away. And we did. We found new recipes. We learned how to cook gluten free—GF—as our daughter figured out she has celiac disease. The rest of us would eat mostly GF, but she stayed the course. And she started feeling so much better.

We just kept learning, experimenting with recipes, becoming better shoppers, and exploring many new markets to shop at. We were all in. And we felt better. Along the way, I had started walking most days of the week. We lived in Minnesota, and the winters were cold. Actually, they were freezing. I hated to be out in the cold, so exercise decreased for about 5+ months. I decided at that point, I needed a way to make me go out each day no matter the weather. After some convincing talks with my husband, we bought a Goldendoodle and named him Andy. And I had my accountability partner!

My nutrition was thriving. My exercise was consistent. My lifestyle was running smoothly. And then some changes in our life were introduced to our family. We moved to Indy; and eighteen months later, we moved to Florida. And two years later, I experienced the first symptoms that led me to make a GI doctor's appointment.

Good Priorities Lead to Better Outcomes

When I received the news and the subsequent plan of care was surgery, I knew I had to zero in on the two things I could control: what I was eating and the amount of movement I was doing. I reached out to a naturopath, Tanda Cook, and started working with her. More in-depth information about what she taught me will be in the section about Restoration. She gave me a specific plan for my nutrition, and I obeyed her instructions to the letter.

I also reached out to another friend, Kari, who is wicked smart. We have been friends for a long time, and her brain works differently from mine. She understands the minutia and can explain the biological details easily, where I get it, but can't always explain the minute details. So, I picked her brain, and she taught me about the process of prolonged fasting. I want to clarify a disclaimer around fasting; you need to consult your PCP before you do any fasting longer than twelve hours overnight. Your PCP knows your specific medical information and can guide you. I know my specific health details; and, having a nursing background, I listened to my friend and bought the books she recommended. I always go back to qualified advice that is backed up by credible research. Kari gave me both. Why did I do prolonged fasting? It is because it helps reset your immune system. And I knew going into surgery and possible chemotherapy, I wanted my immune system to be in the best shape it has ever been.

After my surgery, I was given the news that I had cancer, which had spread to three lymph nodes. I knew that was not great news; but as a new student in oncology, I would soon learn that three lymph nodes are not a lot. And as I put some pieces together, I want to share my hypothesis; I want you to know that this is a hypothesis, not a proven fact. I will get the truth only after I reach Jesus and He gives me the perfect answer.

My Puzzle Pieces:

- Polyp/tumor had been growing for a long time, per my surgeon
- Polyp/tumor was about 5 cm in diameter
- Three Lymph nodes affected out of the 16 my surgeon removed

I have a hypothesis:

If my tumor had been growing for a "long time" and had only spread to three lymph nodes, did the fact I had been eating a whole-food, plant-based diet, walking every day, experiencing a good sleep pattern, and consuming quality supplements help play a part? If I had continued to eat the "Standard American Diet," not exercised consistently, and not taken quality supplements, would I have experienced a different spread of cancer? These are questions I can't answer fully, but I do ponder a lot about them. There is a lot of research, and I keep reading to find out more.

I have boiled it down to this. A whole-foods, plant-based food choices, and minimal sugar is backed by research as the best thing we can do to add to our health journey. Regular exercise is also supported by research as beneficial for minimizing all diseases. What you put on your skin is also essential as our skin absorbs everything we put on it. Pay attention to what is in your bathroom as the ingredients in your products for your hair and skin also matter.

The research on supplements is all over the board. I am providing my view on supplements—they are the "icing on the cake" of our health journey. If you choose to take supplements after consulting with your PCP/healthcare team, ensure they are high quality, meaning they are bio-available. Bio-available means that, as they are digested, they are absorbed into your cells. It does your body no good to swallow pills that stay intact throughout your GI system and end up in the sewer. And quality companies have research on their products that show what is available. These details are way above my pay grade, but I have seen the studies on various products. Please be very intentional in your research and ask for the details of the supplements you purchase.

As I learned that first day with my surgeon, even if we do everything correctly, disease can still occur...and does. It is still worth it to do the right things. It is better to have your body fueled with the most nutrients so it can be the strongest; if a disease starts, our bodies can defeat it or most likely stunt its growth. None of this is guaranteed; but I fully believe, as a nurse, it is our responsibility to make the best choices. And because I put my health as a high priority in my life, along with having a purpose of sharing about the importance of our health, I believe it has had a positive impact.

I have shared how I learned some important priorities as I watched my Grandpa go through his aortic valve replacement, my husband's bout of swine flu, and my learning steps of different eating styles. You have had your own journey. You also may be contemplating some new ideas as you read this and other books. Education and observation are a few of the many ways to further our learning. What is important to note is that, the more you learn, the better decisions you will make moving forward. If you are looking to refine your priorities and purpose, I hope reading these chapters is giving you some items to reflect on and clarify the steps you want to take as you walk into the future.

Questions to Journal

Are you satisfied with your priorities? If not, what do you want to address in your priority list?

Are you living your life on purpose? Has your purpose changed recently or do you feel like you are at a point where your purpose may be taking a new direction? If so, take some time to explore your next steps.

What healthy choices have I put off because of the attitude, "Why should I eat healthy because I am going to die anyway?"

_____

_____

_____

_____

_____

_____

_____

_____

_____

_____

_____

CHAPTER 9

INTENTION—LIVE LIFE OUT LOUD

"I have told you this so that my joy may be in you and that your joy may be complete. My command is this: Love each other as I have loved you. Greater love has no one than this that he lay down his life for his friends. You are my friends if you do what I command."

JOHN 15:11-14 NIV

When you circle your wagons to gather support, your friends from nursing school shoot straight to the top. I reached out, shared my story, and we created a text group. We didn't have this "luxury" when we were in college. And I honestly think our nursing professors are more than thankful for the lack of technology in the 1990s. It was bad enough to be asked to give the lecture as I was generally the one guilty of talking during those lectures, oops. That's the first glance into our group. We were tight and there were not many moments of silence...even during our nursing lectures.

This is our group—Lisa, Teresa, Angie, Deb, and I. We each came excited to the College of Nursing as we all wanted to be the best nurses. We each had a differing focus. Deb wanted to take care of babies, Angie and Teresa wanted to be in the OR, Lisa wanted to take care of Critical Care, and I was an L/D nurse all the way. But before we could do that, we needed to pass Anatomy, Pathophysiology, Pharmacology, and all those nursing classes. And all those hours as nursing assistants and nursing students in the hallowed halls of the University of Iowa Hospitals and Clinics is where we put our book knowledge into practice. We were focused, studied together, and made sure each of us knew it all. We were not allowing anyone to slack or miss out on any points of learning.

This meant many hours in the health/science library, rotating between our apartments and the lounge of the School of Nursing to learn and teach each other along the way. Who knew that Cheerios floating in milk is a great way to "picture" the difference between hemoglobin and hematocrit. You get pretty punchy the longer you study together about every detail of a human body. We were together for every class and most clinical rotations. And just for the fun of it, I got married at the start of our team forming and managed to have a baby during the Spring Break of our Senior year. We experienced it all, and the memories are priceless as we still giggle about the fun we had.

We went our different directions after we graduated. Promising to keep in touch and get together soon. For a variety of reasons, we weren't fantastic about getting together. Keeping in touch is much easier with texting for sure. And as I got the details of my diagnosis, I knew this group would rally together and the team would provide love and strength to carry me through. And they have and continue to do so.

As my treatment continued, we made a plan for them to come down after I finished treatment to celebrate a victory over conquering colon cancer. We set the date, made the plans, and all the details for an epic reunion. We came up with a theme—Golden Girls. Perfect as we had all reached the goal of fifty years old. T-shirts were made and the cheesecake was to be baked. If you have watched the classic TV series "The Golden Girls," you know why cheesecake and gathering in Florida are key details. This would be the first time we would be together in twenty-seven years, so we were going all out in the event planning department. A friend offered up their beach condo for us to stay at, and we called this a perfect plan.

They landed on a Thursday afternoon and promised that, even though they flew together, they would replay the conversations for me so I didn't miss out on anything. And as you can guess, we didn't stop talking the whole time. Our weekend was surrounded by the food we ate, the wine choices that they enjoyed, and the views from sunrise to sunset; and we basically replayed our lives to catch each other up on everything that had happened since 1994.

There is a quote that says, "The best memories are created when gathered around a table." And there is a lot of truth in that. Grab some food, pull up a chair, put on some "Yacht Rock" from Spotify, and let the memories unfold. For us, it truly was going around the table and starting from the day we graduated and sharing our families' stories. This was the best. The details of the different stages of our families, the stories that touched our hearts as we heard about each child as they grew up, and those times we each experienced were moments that took our breath away, but ultimately created the strongest bonds in our friendships. With each story that was shared, we each were brought into each other's closest family moments and our bonds strengthened.

The conversations continued each sunrise and through each sunset as we strolled the beach. There is something special about the waves gently kissing the beach shore and the salty air as it enters your lungs. It clears your mind and soothes the soul. We let that happen and just dove deeper into our conversations. There is something special about the people that are in the innermost circle of your life. Twenty-seven years had passed, but we were still connected as if we were sitting in those auditorium seats for lecture.

It was the BEST TIME EVER. And we have the pictures to keep the joy alive and the smiles radiant.

In one of the many conversations that we had, Angie looked at all of us and informed us that at the beginning of the year she had chosen the word *Intentional*. And when I shared my diagnosis, she knew that her commitment to her word of 2021 was making sure that she came to Florida no matter what. They each lived out this word—more not only for this weekend, but since the moment we formed our friendship. Being intentional literally means *deliberate* according to Oxford Languages. I know we would do the same for each of us in the group, no matter the circumstance. We are connected to endure all types of "weather" in our lives.

During our weekend as we talked and caught up, it hit me. We had all lived our lives "out loud."

There are so many people trying to live picture-perfect lives. People want the perfect filter on their selfies—ok, I may be guilty of this sometimes, LOL. But so many people want their lives to appear to be without fault. Everything seems just too good to be true. Their careers are going straight to the top, and their families could easily be featured in social media influencers "hall of fame" because they appear to be picture perfect.

I want to look at this from a different angle. The cultural lens of "perfection" is so shallow and fleeting. Our cultural view is full of sin, lust, pride, and the distraction of the devil. Living our lives "out loud" can be so many things. All of these things can make this world a better place, not just a pretty picture with a lot of "likes." We all have specific gifts to bring to each relationship. And if you refer back to the Scripture verse at the beginning of this chapter, you will see some simple and profound commands given by Jesus about friendship. Jesus is the ultimate friend.

Love Each Other as I Have Loved You

It seems so simple. Love each other as I have loved you. But it is far from simple, if we forget the first commandment that Jesus reminded us of in

Matthew 22:37-40 NIV, "Jesus replied, 'Love the Lord your God with all your heart and with all your soul and with all your mind.' This is the first and greatest commandment. And the second is like it: 'Love your neighbor as yourself.' All the Law and the Prophets hang on these two commandments."

Don't miss the detail. We are to love God, first, so that we can love each other. This is a key detail. This truth is there for us to be pointed to the most important relationship. Our relationship with God is the forerunner to all of our earthly relationships. Without a relationship with our Father in heaven, our relationships on earth will not happen as they should. Look around. Are we loving our neighbors and each other as Jesus has described? Do a quick scroll through your personal relationships. How are you loving everyone on your list? How are you loving your enemies? That command is in Matthew 5:43-48.

There are so many examples in the Gospels—Matthew, Mark, Luke, and John. Jesus lived a perfect life and exhibited so many examples in those four books of the Bible. Many more were not recorded as they couldn't include every detail of Jesus' ministry. As John says in John 21:25 NIV, "Jesus did many other things as well. If every one of them were written down, I suppose that even the whole world would not have room for the books that would be written." I encourage you to take much time to study them over your life.

But for now, let's focus on a few things that are important in loving each other. What are some basics of a relationship? Most relationships start because you find a common interest; another is that it is easy to talk with someone, and one that creates a level of trust that is not done easily—being vulnerable.

Common Interest

When we start a conversation with someone, we usually ask the same "surface" questions:

- Are you married?

- Do you have kids?
- What do you do for a living?
- How long have you lived here? Or, Where did you grow up?

They are usually safe questions to ask, they don't cause us to commit too much, and they make us appear friendly. They are good questions for social situations, but they are so predictable. And sometimes that is appropriate. Not everyone we meet is supposed to be our best friend.

There is a time in some conversations when either you are asked a question that goes a step further, or you ask the question of your new acquaintance that inquires further into a favorite hobby or how they contribute to the community. And then it comes to light! You both look at each other and have discovered a commonality and something that brings you close enough to exchange information and schedule a time to connect further.

In life, we usually have a few layers of relationships. They go from the inner circle, close friends, a few layers of friends, and then to the outer circle of acquaintances. Each circle has an important function in our lives. It doesn't matter if you claim you are an extrovert or an introvert. We all have friends in these circles. Not everyone has an overflowing "black book" of friends, but I want to focus on developing the quality of your relationships.

Vulnerability

For some of you that means letting a few more people into the closer circles of your life. It doesn't mean that you share everything with everyone. It does mean that you open yourself up a little more with a few more people. I shared earlier that it was a process for me to share my cancer diagnosis more broadly. It may be similar for you with yourself. But the difference with relationships you have already established is it can be easier to open a little bit more with those with whom you are already somewhat familiar. We are built to be in relationship with others. And when we are a little bit more open with others, they will reciprocate.

When you both share a little more, the ripple effect will go further than just the two of you. More relationships will get deeper because we won't just open up a little more with just one person. We tend to then extend our circles, and our deeper understanding of each person creates a friendlier world overall.

Opening up to someone and developing a deeper relationship with others doesn't mean you are laying your whole life out for each other. Most of the time it is just finding a little bit more about their interests or a few more questions about their family career, or hobbies. People generally enjoy talking about themselves. So ask a few more questions about them and listen. Listen to understand, not to simply reply. Remember an additional detail about that person, and then ask about it the next time you are together. Be sincere as you get to know them better. It took me longer than most to understand this concept, but it has truly changed the relationships I now have. Most times, as I meet someone, I frequently have reached the point quickly where we exchange phone numbers so we can connect again. I have found that we all are seeking a little closer connection with others. We need each other and being able to know someone a little closer is indescribable over the long run.

Jesus' command boils down to the word I have used to start off the chapters in this section—intention or intentional. Loving relationships are intentional. You don't have an agenda, but you are prepared and thoughtful. You go the extra mile to be more available, more real, more open, more everything as the relationship grows.

Some people take relationships for granted. They open up only partially. They check in only when absolutely necessary. They believe that relationship is deep, but really desire only the surface things to be discussed. I have heard this many times—we don't want to ask too many questions or, the most famous one, that's none of our business. Hold it? Really? If that's your usual pattern, I encourage you to make changes soon. Ask one question that goes a little deeper and get to know someone a little bit more this week.

I have been on both sides of this next relationship mishap. We ask people how they are—and what does everyone reply 95% of the time? "I am fine." We all know that response is mostly untrue. But, I have done it myself. I have lied when things were falling apart either because it was not the right moment to share more or because I wasn't ready to be authentic. Either way, it wasn't the best choice. There are moments even in our closest relationships that we pull back into our "shells" instead of taking a breath to be open and have a deeper conversation. It doesn't mean it will be a fight; it means we will need to share, listen, be open to the feedback, etc. It's interesting, some people fear even the most normal conversations. They live in their "shells" and give as little as they can to maintain a relationship. It's intriguing to see how people live in their different relationships. There may be some things dwelling from their past that they may or may not ever surface. Being more observant with our interactions will help us build more authentic relationships with everyone we connect with.

We are called to love each other. And that means to love each other where they are. It also means to build a stronger relationship with them along the way. That may look entirely different with each person. It is the symbiotic give and take of our lives. My nursing friends are part of my inner circle, even though we aren't family and don't see each other frequently. We established the foundation of our friendship over the 2 ½ years as we studied nursing. The time in between contact and the distance between our homes haven't unraveled the foundation. Relationships that are trustworthy, authentic, and safe are avenues that help us be able to live our lives out loud. We can be authentic with all because we have strong relationships.

Living out loud in our relationships has multiple levels. However, the impact that we can have with more people as we lean in and learn more about others will have an unlimited effect in all areas of everyone's life. Giving a little more of yourself to someone or a few someones will make this world a little more connected. When we are more connected, we understand each other more, and that leads to greater understanding across your relationships.

From your small circle to a large group, these tips and others will help improve all relationships.

Questions to Journal

After reviewing your relationships, have you picked a few with whom you want to explore growing deeper?

Another way to deepen relationships is to connect others. Invite out for coffee a few friends of yours who don't know each other, but have similar interests. See what grows.

What is the hardest part for you as you have built relationships? What do you need to do to be more open in your closest relationships?

Is there someone you know who would be a great mentor to help you in growing other relationships in your life?

_____

_____

_____

_____

_____

_____

_____

_____

_____

CHAPTER 10

INTENTION—DISEASE DOESN'T FOLLOW THE RULES

"Consequently, just as the result of one trespass was condemnation for all men, so also the result of one act of righteousness was justification that brings life for all men. For just as through the disobedience of the one man the many were made sinners, so also through the obedience of the one man the many will be made righteous."

ROMANS 5:18-19 NIV

Not today, Satan. Not today.

Not in a whisper. Not in your inside voice.

Say it with your Easter voice as a Pastor proclaims, "HE IS RISEN!"

And the congregation responds joyfully, "HE IS RISEN INDEED! HALLELUJAH!"

Declare it! Declare it with Godfidence—**NOT TODAY, SATAN! NOT TODAY!**

Or as David stood before Goliath, he stood there with the confidence of God.

He had a stone and a slingshot—one chance.

He killed Goliath.

"As that giant was looking at us, I knew he was going to regret the day he was pointing the sword at 'us.' Just as Goliath pointed the sword at David, the sword Goliath pointed at David became the sword that the little boy picked up, and took the giant's head off with," Bethel Music introduction to 'Raise a Hallelujah.'[1]

The devil introduced sin into this world in Genesis Chapter 3. And from that point on, sin crept into and has been expressed through all of creation—all people, weeds, death, pain in childbirth, and of course, disease. The devil has been battling to win us over ever since. He plans to twist the truth just slightly for us to follow him. That is exactly how he deceived Eve; he twisted God's truth just a little. There is a spiritual battle each day of our lives. We make a choice every second to follow the devil or God. Each second, the devil will work to distract us from the love of God. Our confident battle cry is this—NOT TODAY, SATAN. NOT TODAY.

It is never good when the devil is guiding your life or the life of someone you love. Some parts look appealing, which is why you or your loved one followed along with the devil's invitation; but then it gets worse. It always does when you let the devil lead the way. Some people's lives don't look horrible as they follow the devil; but as you watch, you note one different thing—they are always searching for something more. I have shared books about faith formation in the Resources section at the back of this book which are all good to read. They are about the life journeys of three different people. I will let them shed light on how they worked through their struggles with a life influenced by the devil.

Most people think of the apparent wrong steps—sexual sin, murder, lying, etc. I want to focus on disease, which goes back to original sin. All sin goes back to the Garden of Eden and the first sin by Adam and Eve.

When my surgeon said, "Disease doesn't follow the rules," he wasn't making any faith-based connection. However, I did after he said it. I knew all things that go wrong in our health and life go back to the original sin. No one asks to have an illness diagnosed, or to have something go wrong after making bad choices. But they both do.

Let's unpack the things that most likely cause and some that may be linked to causing disease. When you look at it through the introduction and see it through to the exponential side effects and chronic diseases, you see how the devil works. Yes, the devil is "in" the details of what we consume and the activities we do or don't do. Everything seems good in the beginning. The "new thing" appears to be reasonable and correct. And then the foundation of the "new thing" seems to fall apart. The longer it is around and research is done, the more of what was initially provided isn't supported by new information. And we have all paid the price in one way or the other.

This is the first tweak I have made to my surgeon's sentence:

**Disease doesn't follow the rules, and we all pay
the price because of original sin.**

Dang! The addition to my surgeon's original sentence is a hard truth, but it's right. I would like to take credit for it, but that was the inspiration of the Holy Spirit. We all pay the price of original sin, even if we don't want to admit it—every one of us feels the pain of each sin. We experience it personally or through the repercussions of our loved ones' choices. We all feel it. And it is never easy.

Major links to cancer, per Mayo Clinic [2]

- Smoking
- Excessive drinking
- Excessive sun exposure, frequent blistering of the skin
- Obesity (i.e., poor diet and lack of exercise)
- Unsafe sex
- Environment—secondhand smoke, chemicals in your home/workplace
- Older age >65
- Family history, a small portion

Most of these things have one thing in common. Like the devil tempting Eve by twisting the truth, most of these things above started off sounding really good.

- Just try a cigarette once...
- Let's go out and have one drink...
- Let's go soak up some sun on the beach...
- Let's grab some doughnuts on the break table...our patients are THE BEST!
- Let's go to my place...
- Baby powder is the BEST!

Sound familiar? Have you fallen for one or all of these? We all have fallen for one or most. And now, some of us are paying the price in one way or the other.

The advertisements we watch on TV or hear on the radio don't disclose the negatives. They don't shout out the long-term side effects of using each product. They don't quote the research that reveals what is negatively affecting our health about their product(s). The actors don't seem to have experienced the long-term effects of the product commercials they are being paid to act in. Hmmm. Are the advertising companies lying to us? Not blatantly, but they twist the truth just like the devil did in Genesis Chapter 3. They show a pretty girl sipping on their product or an athletic guy handing his football helmet to a young boy. And as the camera fades, he takes a sip of the product. Great music in the background, effective lighting, and the words were carefully chosen.

And the next time we are at the grocery store, if it is not that product in our carts, it's all the others. We buy them, we consume them, and they make more money. It is a vicious cycle. The ingredients that are in these products feed that cycle. If we don't have more, we get a headache, don't have enough pep, and "need" our fix. These companies have created an addiction in most Americans. And then eventually, three years, five years, ten years down the road, we go to the doctor's office to have our annual physicals. And while we are there, we discover or have to admit we have a laundry list of problems or symptoms. We have a choice—a pill or two, or to make some changes in our lives? The latter being an option which will let our body heal from the inside out.

Company X doesn't share in their commercials that you will gain weight and experience all the side effects, chronic diseases, and possible links to cancer. Those football players in their commercials are robust and healthy, though. The "funny" thing is when people quit using Company X's products, they lose weight, decrease or stop needing their chronic disease meds, have more energy, and don't have brain fog anymore. The list of problems that disappear when we remove one product can change many things in our body. Now think about what your body would feel like and how efficient it would function if you didn't take in ANY processed foods?

Processed foods of EVERY variety have increased the footprint of every grocery store in America and around the world. When I grew up, we had a tiny corner size grocery store. It had fresh produce, a meat counter, a few baked goods, and a small selection of canned goods, cereals, and boxed goods. I think the women, back in the day, would have scoffed at a large selection of pre-made pies, rolls, cookies, and cakes to purchase in a grocery store! That's what an excellent Lutheran cookbook is for. We baked everything from scratch! Most researchers and doctors will say that if you make it at home, it is better than processed. They will admit that the amount of sugar we use as we bake is far less than the combination of the amount of sugar, preservatives, and artificial ingredients in processed foods. The previous recommendation does not give you the freedom to make an excessive amount of sweets at home and declare yourself "healthy." It means that baking something homemade and eating it occasionally will have a lessened effect on creating chronic diseases than eating processed foods day in and day out. The words are called moderation and occasional, not a unending buffet of junk food.

Do I purchase processed foods? Minimally. The short list is GF pasta, spaghetti sauce, GF crackers or chips (rarely), GF muffin or cornbread mixes (rarely), and a few condiments. If you see me in the grocery store, my cart has a lot of fresh produce and things from the store's periphery. We all enjoy cooking and baking, so our pantry is full of staples, not boxes, bags, and cans. And soon, a raised-bed vegetable garden is coming to our side yard. I am excited to learn how to grow veggies and herbs here in Florida! I continue to embrace what Tanda has taught me every step I take—know thy farmer.

There Is A Chasm—How Do We Resist Temptations?

This is an age-old question. I don't have the complete answer, but I will share some things that have helped guide me through my life. We all need boundaries. The problem is we want to create boundaries that let us "cheat" a little bit. We think others' limits are too restrictive. I will drop some truth here for all of us—yes, I preach to myself as I type. We are all sinful, and our version of boundaries is cracked. They are not going to keep us on the straight and narrow. Anything we "right" is going to benefit us, and only us. There were ten commandments written by God himself and handed to Moses. And if you read Exodus and throughout the Bible, you will see how humans messed up and extended the commandments afterwards. They tried to have laws for every situation, which muddied the waters and caused many problems.

In my humble opinion, we should go back to the original ten. Read them.

The Ten Commandments.

1. Thou shalt have no other gods before me.
2. Thou shalt not make unto thee any graven image.
3. Thou shalt not take the name of the Lord thy God in vain.
4. Remember the Sabbath day to keep it holy.
5. Honor thy Father and thy Mother.
6. Thou shalt not kill.
7. Thou shalt not commit adultery.
8. Thou shalt not steal.
9. Thou shalt not bear false witness against thy neighbor.
10. Thou shalt not covet. [3]

The United States has anywhere from 10,000–50,000 laws, depending on what source you access on Google. And our Legislative branch of government is still trying to add more to make us safer and prevent all conceivable "things." At any point in our country, these laws passed and in the future are never going to prevent sin from occurring. And that is why the Constitution is another well-written document. It is encompassing but not "in the weeds." If you haven't read it. You should.

When the laws of our country (a number that is not quantifiable because of our local, state, and federal branches) are compared to the commandments, the ten commandments are more simplified. I am a simple girl. I will take the ten commandments in a heartbeat. Why? There are ten. And they cover all the bases. Re-read them if you need to. They encompass all parts of our lives. These ten commandments provide detail to help us prevent all problems, but the reality is that no one keeps all of the commandments. News flash, we have all broken EVERY commandment. It turns out that even if you lust after a man or think about killing someone, you have broken those commandments. We needed Jesus to be the perfect sacrifice. We still need Jesus to help us walk through this earthly life. We are completely sinful.

The Ten Commandments are GENIUS! I have them posted in one of our bathrooms above the toilet. I have had many wonderful conversations with our boys. It turns out they read as they carry out their business. (Free parenting tip for you.) These commandments are why you are reading this book and how I have ordered it. The information is general but has a specific impact. I can't and won't describe how to be healthy and live as lengthy of a life as God grants to us in micro-detail. I also won't promise changes in thirty days. That would be fraudulent and false advertising.

Do our bodies feel and change the first day we implement healthy habits? Yes. How do I know this? Our bodies are built out of many, many cells—37.2 trillion to be exact. [4] When we take a deep breath, we give our bodies more oxygen. Our cells are the first recipients of that increased oxygen and respond accordingly. Let's take it to the next level. What happens when we go for a walk? Every cell is affected—cardiovascular, muscular, brain, etc. They start the repair process immediately. It's that simple. Every good decision creates a domino effect of healing or restoring homeostasis. The reverse is true. Each wrong decision you make opens up your body to disease and illness. More will be covered in the next section.

But Why Make Healthy Choices?

There are always two sides to the discussion. Let's ask more questions and discuss some answers. Most questions when we want to give into temptation are rooted in emotions, because we are "addicted" to the temptation. I have been there and still can be tempted; we are all human. Answers to the most commonly verbalized questions will be based in facts and research.

Why should we make healthy choices?

- Why can't I enjoy those processed foods, the sodas, the beers I enjoy each evening, etc.?

- These extra pounds I weigh are not that big of a problem, are they?
- Why does everyone worry about my health?
- Isn't it my health, not theirs?
- I thought you said that God has our days numbered, so why does it matter what I eat or how much I exercise?
- I know someone who ate "this way" and is fine. They have no illness or diseases.
- My family health history is impeccable. I shouldn't have to worry about X.

These questions bring up some important points.

- Actions have consequences.
- The research does not support processed foods for any part of our health. More information in Chapter 12 for all research-based nutrition answers.
- The extra pounds will put anyone at an increased rate for all chronic illnesses and diseases. For every ten pounds that you lose, it will decrease your risk.
- The healthcare costs incurred for any chronic illness or disease, both out-of-pocket and insurance premium cost, impacts everyone.
- Chronic illnesses and diseases have consequences which impact more than each individual.
- If you have kept yourself healthy, when illness or disease does "break-in," your body will be stronger and have a better chance at defeating the disease or illness.
- If you have any conditions (high BMI, high BP, Diabetes 1 or 2, or cardiac conditions) that put you at risk, your body may not be able to defend itself as robustly when the disease enters.
- The effects on all areas of your life if you have a disease:
  - How will it affect your family?
  - How will it impact your job?

- How will it affect your finances?
- How will it affect your energy?
- How will the medications affect you, and what about the side effects?

- Healthy eating and consistent exercise are part of the free will that God gave us, and this leads to healthier days that he has appointed to you.

- Genetics does play a part in our health along with our eating and activity choices; no one is guaranteed the same outcome as someone else they know.

- No matter your family history, sometimes we each can be diagnosed with something that has not been genetically involved in our family history.

Temptations surround us every second of our day; they all come from the devil. They are disguised as tasty treats and drinks, sexual enjoyment outside of marriage, time in front of the TV, computer, or our phones, and a stop at a local bar for a few drinks with friends/co-workers. It starts with one of these or a few others that I have not mentioned. The first time doesn't look bad, and we may not get "caught." But then, a second, or a third, and twenty years later—a diagnosis finds us sitting in an office with a large polyp in our colon. My surgeon said, "That has been growing in your colon FOR YEARS." I am a product of original sin; I have given in to temptations; and on that day, I had the disease in my body—mic drop.

The sentence, "Disease does not follow the rules," has been rolling in my mind since my surgeon shared it. But every time I heard it, there seemed to be an incompleteness about it. It is true when we say disease doesn't follow the rules. To me, it felt as though there should be more. On one of my walks, I kept asking God if there was supposed to be something more. I had this tug in my gut which kept nagging at me to put a comma where my surgeon had placed a period. Disease doesn't follow the rules, but God. But God what, I kept thinking. And then God clarified it for me.

Disease doesn't follow the rules, but God _____.

The line is for God to fill in for EACH person. There is ALWAYS a "but God" in each of our messy situations. His response is personal to each of our situations. God meant for there to be a comma so give Him the glory as we see Him work the perfect solution for our situations or diagnoses. He overcame my cancer and all diseases at the cross. Jesus said, "It is finished." Not only was His life finished, but the everlasting effects of our sins were forgiven at that moment.

We need to let Him show up in our mess and write our story. We can then finish the sentence with the perfect details that God has shown us as He completes our story. When disease doesn't follow the rules, God shows up and perfects our outcomes/stories.

We have explored many things thus far and have started to uncover some areas we have been avoiding putting work into. Journal the following questions and spend time as you let God work on your soul. It is time to move to the restoration phase and allow God to create the "perfect for us" next chapters to our stories.

Questions to Journal

From "New Morning Mercies" by Paul David Tripp, questions from the July 8 entry. [5]

What set of values determines your schedule?

What view of life determines how you make decisions?

What perspective about the nature of and purpose for your existence forms your everyday street-level priorities?

How does your thinking shape what you do and say every day?

_____

_____

_____

_____

_____

_____

_____

_____

_____

_____

_____

CHAPTER 11

RESTORATION IN YOUR EMOTIONS AND MINDSET

"Rejoice in the Lord always. I will say it again: Rejoice! Let your gentleness be evident to all. The Lord is near. Do not be anxious about anything but in everything, by prayer and petition, with thanksgiving, present your requests to God. And the peace of God, which transcends all understanding, will guard your hearts and your minds in Christ Jesus.

Finally, brothers, whatever is true, whatever is noble, whatever is right, whatever is pure, whatever is lovely, whatever is admirable—if anything is excellent or praiseworthy—think about such things. Whatever you have learned or received or heard from me, or seen in me—put it into practice. And the God of peace will be with you."

PHILIPPIANS 4:4-9 NIV

> "Peace I leave with you; my peace I give you. I do not give to you as the world gives. Do not let your hearts be troubled and do not be afraid."
>
> JOHN 14:27 NIV

Fair warning. This chapter will be rough and treacherous for some. I am going to be jumping up and down on the edge of some of your comfort zones, and you may toss this book in the corner in frustration. That's ok. Sometimes you have to walk away when someone confronts you with your blind spot if you are not ready to deal with it right now. BUT...come back. The biggest hurdle we all have is in our minds. It can play some significant tricks on us. It can warp our perception of all areas of our lives. It can lead us down some destructive paths. It can take us to the brink of taking our own life. That is why it is the first chapter of this section as we discuss restoration. If we don't work on this first, the rest will never fall "neatly" into place. Trust me on this.

I have had some personal experiences in "jumping on" my comfort zone and exposure to my blind spots. Those are days you never forget. Those experiences are not something you can prepare for in advance. When someone confronts you, it is usually in the "midst." If it happens in person, you will be making a choice face to face with someone helping you change your life trajectory. I have had it happen a few times during phone conversations with my friend, Patty. She is a master at listening and picking up on cues. And she has a thoughtful way of wording her "teachings" to you. I have hung up on her a few times as she candidly pointed out a few of my blind spots—and it hurt. It is not easy to hear the truth about your choices or behavior. BUT every time, she was right. When you have strong relationships with wise people, you listen and take to heart the hard teachings they share. As I write going forward, you may have that same feeling. I won't claim that I am the wisest person in the room. I know I am not. I am a work in progress; however, I have learned enough to help you change the trajectory of your life as you read this book. These hard truths are better to read now and work on soon, then to ignore and continue down the wrong path.

It's not just our minds; the devil specializes in manipulating our thoughts if we are not prepared with the truth of Jesus Christ. We can't play with the devil alone and win. Jesus already won the ultimate battle with the devil. Jesus defeated the devil on the cross, meaning that all who believe in Jesus will experience trials on earth; but we have the guarantee of eternal life with Jesus in heaven. We have not been left alone. We have been given the gift of the Holy Spirit as believers, so we have a counselor to help us every step of our lives.

Full disclosure. I am in this battle with the devil each day, right alongside you. I have no special privileges or power. As you read this book, in chapter 1, my mindset had tumbled, and I have flailed just like you. Life can come at each and every one of us and blow us over, no matter the amount of faith we have in Jesus. But, we also have the choice to repent and get back up, stronger than before.

Before you read any further, stop. Close your eyes. Pray. Do not skip this step. Let's dig in.

I want to go deeper into the story I shared in the first chapter, about having a tough time accepting I had a large polyp, especially after eating well and exercising consistently. I had a great struggle accepting I had to have surgery to remove a section of my colon. My mind was in a state of indignation—defined in the Oxford Dictionary of English as "anger or annoyance provoked by what is perceived as an unfair treatment." [1] I completely understand that life is not fair, BUT I was in a spot mentally that was feeling thoroughly cheated. And I was so lost in my own "hurricane" that it took me a good chunk of time to get out of said hurricane and be able to let God heal my mind.

In the meantime, my surgeon and a few other close people took the brunt of my emotions and actions. Those close to me who knew me before my hurricane weathered my storm and knew I could come out ok because they knew God was my focus. My surgeon had no clue who I was and possibly thought he should be writing a psych eval after that encounter the day after surgery, and for sure after my port post-op follow-up appointment. He saw only a snapshot of my life.

So let's stop there and take a moment to look at something. We know people on a variety of levels. And that can help us be an anchor or a flotation device in their lives. My surgeon could have been an anchor in my life, if he had intervened the way some medical providers may have as they looked at my poor interactions with him. But, he listened to me and saw my actions; and I felt he believed in me when I was flailing in the middle of my storm. Each time we talked, I heard him say something that helped me look forward in hope as he shared something about the next steps in my plan of care. God bless him for caring for me in my hurricane. I was a complete mess.

Because my family and friends knew my whole story, they could come alongside me, listen to my saga, and pray. Rarely did anyone try to solve my problem, and I learned a lot as I observed their interactions with me. I am a nurse and have wanted to solve everyone's problems for the last 28 years of my life. I felt that was my job. That's not always helpful. I was brought back to the example of a chick pecking its way out of its eggshell or a butterfly emerging from its cocoon. If we help them emerge faster, they will likely die. If we let them do the work, they will emerge stronger and prepared for the rest of their life.

That's what we are going to explore fully in this chapter. I want to help you peck your way out of your eggshell. I am not going to tell you what to do. I will throw out some suggestions occasionally to help you think outside of your box; but more often, I will pose many questions for you to ponder. There is a list of books in the Resources section for you to read if you so choose. These books will also help you look inside and see that there may be a thing or two for you to work on. I also stumbled upon a list of questions to "Find your Passion" that is in the resource section. This chapter focuses on putting on your boots and getting to work. Are you ready?

Before We Heal, We Have to Admit There Is Something Wrong—Ouch!

I encourage you to look at two devotionals as you read this section.

"New Morning Mercies" by Paul David Tripp, the writing for the day of June 15.

"Confession is not natural for us. It's natural for us to think of ourselves as more righteous than we are. It's natural to blame our wrongs on others. It's natural to say our behavior was caused by some difficult circumstance we were in. It's natural to exercise our inner lawyers and defend ourselves when we're confronted with a sin, weakness, or failure. It's natural to turn the tables when being confronted and tell our accusers that they are surely bigger sinners than we are. It's natural to see ourselves more as law keepers than as law breakers. It's natural to point to our biblical literacy or theological knowledge as proof of our spiritual mastery. It's natural to be more concerned about the sin of others than our own. It's natural to be more critical of the attitudes and behavior of others than our own. It's natural for you and me to be blind to the depth of our spiritual need.

Because this sturdy system of self-righteousness is natural for every sinner, it is unnatural for us to be clear-sighted, humble, self-examining, and ready to confess. Blind eyes and a self-satisfied, self-congratulatory heart stand in the way of the broken heart of confession. We don't grieve our sin because we don't see it. It is ironic that we tend to see the righteousness we don't have and we fail to see the sin that stains every day of our lives.

Here's how confession works. You cannot confess what you haven't grieved, you can't grieve what you do not see, and you cannot repent of what you have not confessed. So one of the most important operations of God's grace is to give us eyes to see our sin and hearts that are willing to confess it. If your eyes are open and you see yourself with accuracy, and if your heart is humbly willing to admit to what your eyes see, you know that glorious, rescuing, forgiving, and transforming grace has visited you. Why? Because what you're doing is simply not natural for sinners. In the face of their sin, Adam blamed Eve, Eve blamed the Serpent, and both of them hid, but neither stepped forward and made willing and heartfelt confession.

So cry out today for eyes to see, that is, for accurate personal insight. Cry out for the defenses of your heart to come down. Ask God to defeat your fear of being exposed, of being known. Cry for the grace to be willing to stop, look, listen, receive, grieve, confess, and turn. Stand with courage and hope before the searching and exposing mirror of the Word of God, and be unafraid. Stand naked before God and know that all that is exposed has been fully and completely covered by the shed blood of your Savior. Because of him, you don't need to be afraid of your unrighteousness; no it is your delusions of righteousness that are the grave danger." [2]

"Live in Grace, Walk in Love" by Bob Goff, writing for the day of June 16.

Wise People Know the Right Arguments to Lose.

"Why do you look at the speck of sawdust in your brother's eye and pay no attention to the plank in your own eye?" Matthew 7:3.

I grew up in a family where my sister and I didn't get along very well. God's idea of putting us in families wasn't a mistake. It was a terrific idea. It's great having people bring us soup when we're sick and help to rake the leaves. When we're kids, a sibling becomes a built-in playmate to find mischief together. One of the biggest ways families are a gift is how they teach us to disagree with one another. Here's why.

Our families show us that our feelings matter and people are meant to have different perspectives and opinions. We find out early on that sometimes we're right and sometimes we're wrong. We also have the opportunity to learn that, most times, being "right" isn't as important as staying in our relationships. We also learn to say we're sorry and make amends when we've hurt someone's feelings.

All this is a good warm-up for the rest of our lives. We will encounter people we disagree with every day, and Jesus calls us to love those people, not just tolerate them. Jesus never told us to be "right." He told us to be gracious. He told us to love people who disagree with us and to even love our enemies. There are ways to disagree poorly and well, but love knows how to do it right and do it often.

Wise people know the right arguments to lose. The fact is, it's most of them. If it's more important for you to be "right" than to be like Jesus, then it's time to get back to the basics of your faith and your relationships. Good relationships can last a lifetime. Don't let an argument spoil even a few moments.

What plank do you have in your own eye? [3]

Look in the Mirror

I shared above that I knew I had something wrong. That's the first step—admitting we are at fault. Admitting our guilt is not a popular thing to do. I learned a poignant rule of thought from my friend, Patty. She has many pearls in the parenting department, and this one is applicable in all areas of life.

As her kids were experiencing the typical troubles most of our children experience in middle and high school, she would talk about this truth when they would share that a particular problem in their life was "someone else's fault." She would lovingly look at them and share that, if it is someone's fault, we can't fix it. If we own the problem, we have complete control to make the changes and improve our lives. I looked at her and exclaimed, "THAT IS GENIUS!" She taught her kids the value of taking personal responsibility for everything. I have taken that gem, have personally implemented it, and have shared it with our children. I have known my whole life how vital taking personal responsibility is, but how she shared this example drove it to a new level in my life.

This last year or so, I have had "Come to Jesus" talks, as I call them, with myself. I was honest with myself and Jesus. I cried out to Jesus for help. I had lots of discussions with my circle. These talks helped me surface a lot of prayer requests, and solutions came slowly but timely. I had to do the work. God had all the answers, and they arrived at the right time. He is not a genie. Jesus gives us a task, and He performs the miracle as we work. Look at Matthew 9:7 "Then he said to the paralytic, 'Get up, take your mat and go home.' And the man got up and went home."

I get what that person back then with paralysis was probably thinking. Because I had some pretty cantankerous thoughts going through my mind when I received the news of my polyp and was instructed to get a surgeon. I was stunned at the information and the work I was asked to do. BUT…that's what Jesus led me to do when I was diagnosed with a colon polyp. He said, essentially, have surgery and complete the treatment they lay out for you. When presented with a problem—physical or mental—we have work to do, BUT GOD will work the miracle of our healing as we follow His instructions.

Here are some questions for you:

- What in your life is not working for you right now?
- Is it physical or mental? Or both?
- Are you ready to admit it?
- Are you ready to work on it?
- What problem (or person) have you been blaming your current situation or limitation on that you now realize you should take responsibility for after you read that wise truth from Patty?
- Who do you feel comfortable meeting with to work on this change you need to make?

- What are some things in your life you know you need to take responsibility for, but right now is too soon to work on them? Write these down and come back to them SOON.

That last question, I put it there for a reason. There are many things in our lives we don't want to admit are a problem. They are called our "blind spots." I have mine, and they are the hardest ones to work on. Why? Because no one wants to admit we are failing or coming up short in that area. OR, we don't like to acknowledge that we have those thoughts/feelings or have acted upon them. And those are the ones we need to work on soon rather than later.

Let's go to Scripture for a little piece of humble pie.

"Why do you look at the speck of sawdust in your brother's eye and pay no attention to the plank in your own eye? How can you say to your brother, 'Let me take the speck out of your eye,' when all the time there is a plank in your own eye? You hypocrite, first take the plank out of your own eye, and then you will see clearly to remove the speck from your brother's eye," Matthew 7:3-5 (NIV).

At this point, you will feel me jumping on the edge of your comfort zone. I want you to metaphorically, or actually, look in the mirror at yourself. I have done this and will continue to do this myself as I am a major work in progress while here on earth. And when we work on ourselves with the help of Jesus, we will destroy our comfort zones, because that's where we live in darkness. That's where we live in our sins. And when Jesus calls us to "take up our mat," He is shining a light into our darkness and exposing our sins, i.e., the planks in our eyes. Doing this is the HARD WORK that Jesus is asking us to do, BUT He will provide us with each step to our healing. And this is why I provide all the Scripture references that I do. Only His truth will light our path. Fully stated in Psalm 119:105 KJV, "Thy word is a lamp unto my feet, and a light unto my path." Jesus lights our life path, one step at a time. He gives us enough instruction for us to take the next right step.

Think about this: If you could see exactly how your entire life would unfold, would you want to know? I have pondered this question many times since my diagnosis, and I am a definite NO. I do not want to see every detail of my future. WHY? Because I would take a different step to avoid the pain. And if I did that, I would not experience the JOY and what I am supposed to learn in the trial. I would miss the will of God to stay in the safest spot. Looking at ourselves in the mirror and admitting what we need to fix is SO HARD! No one wants to admit their wrongdoing or their wrong thoughts. I sure don't. But we have to. We have to face the pain, make the course corrections, take a new path, and put our focus back on God. And that, my friend, is the hard work of healing—admitting that we are wrong. Make the fix. Change your course. I am going to ask you again. Are you ready?

Let's Heal

I would like to direct you to the devotional reference earlier, "New Morning Mercies" by Paul David Tripp, and to read the devotional for October 16. I would also encourage you to watch the video clip from the movie "Facing the Giants" located on YouTube titled, Facing the Giants—Death Crawl, and Herb Brooks' Miracle Speech—You Were Born for This. Each of these references will be helpful as you work through healing your mindset and your emotions.

My surgeon said five words to me: Disease doesn't follow the rules. Those words changed the trajectory of my healing. He didn't say those to have a life-changing impact on my life. He just stated it to remind me that I wasn't in control of my health. I heard those words like no one else would ever listen to them. They struck a chord so deep in my heart and my gut that I still listen to them in my mind each day. You will have a specific encounter that is meant for you, and it will change the trajectory of your life and health. You will draw that proverbial line in the sand and say, "ENOUGH!" Today is Day One of the rest of my life. I am not going back to how I was living.

You will put down that drink. You will extinguish that cigarette. You will walk away from the drugs. You will leave that soda or that candy on the shelf. You will not repeat the mistakes you have made in that relationship. God will help you do it. Again, we don't do anything on our own. We can claim we are doing it. We can say the "I am" statements. BUT those "I am" statements refer to the great I AM, God. We know that we have to give credit to God. "Jesus looked at them and said, 'With man this is impossible, but with God all things are possible." Matthew 19:26 NIV, Only God, can make what was in shambles new. Only God can create our new path. Give Him credit.

Here are some questions to journal, contemplate, and possibly discuss with a mentor:

- Do you know Jesus?
- Do you need to know Jesus better to let Him heal you?
- Are you ready to take steps to heal fully? Are you prepared to dig down to the root cause of your problems and heal all the way?
- If you are not ready to heal all the way, what is holding you back?
    - Are you scared to pull back the layers?
    - Are you not sure you can make it "through the valleys" during the healing process?
    - Are you not ready to face or take responsibility for your issues/problems?
    - Are you not ready to ask for or get help from God, a healthcare team, or a mental healthcare team?
    - Are you not ready to learn and make the changes?
    - Are you too proud or arrogant? Pride often causes us to avoid correction by blaming our problems on someone else or why we lean on our "crutch."

These questions are not easy. Healing completely is not easy. You need to be ready to lean in and work. This work is going to make you sweat. It is going to make you vulnerable. It is going to make you honest, really honest. Why do we have to do the "hard" work? Because if we don't, we will never be completely healed and be able to live the life God intended for us. If we don't heal, we will continue to have something holding us back. When you dig deep and recover fully, immediately the transformation in your life begins. Without the "check-up from the neck up," as my mentor, Rita Davenport, shared with so many of us at conferences, you will be in the same place next year and every year after. No one wants to stay stuck, but many people don't want to do the work. Do the work. Join me. It's worth it.

Steps to Healing Our Mindset and Emotions—The Basic Level

These steps are going to look different for everyone. We all have various details of what is going on in our mindsets and emotions, and we all engage and learn differently from others. I am offering some ideas from various resources I have become familiar with in my life/career. There may be varying degrees of things available for you in your local area. Best tip: Ask more questions of those you know in your immediate "circle" and of your healthcare team.

Your goal is to heal your mindset and emotions entirely. If the person that you connect with is not making you uncomfortable in the sense of helping you open up and helping you discover what is wrong, please seek other people. I want to clarify a few things. The person you obtain help from should be licensed or certified by credible sources. The person should align with your values. The person should have a plan for healing, i.e., we are going to work together for X months, this is the scope of work we are going to do, and have a plan to "graduate" you out of their care. Most of us do not need ongoing therapy. And the person caring for you should want you to heal completely. If that is not part of their care plan for you, seek care elsewhere. You are not going to someone to have a "gripe" session a few times a week or weekly for the rest of your life. That is not healing.

The person you connect with may be a counselor/mental health practitioner, a Pastor/Priest/Rabbi, or a faith-based counselor. Check with your Employee Assistance Program for possible free meetings with a counselor. Check with your insurance carrier about what is covered or offered through them. Your HR department of your employer should be able to answer all things about coverage and many alternate options available to you. That is your choice. You want someone with whom you can be honest, natural, and authentic. You also have to commit to being receptive to the feedback, suggestions to be implemented, and the process of growth they will be taking you through.

A health coach is also great to work with on your mindset, emotions, nutrition, and exercise. Health coaches work privately, through insurance companies, and possibly through a third party through your employer. Ask around your community and your HR department for their availability. They can be valuable as you look at the team you are forming to have the most optimal health journey.

This process should help you create a new mindset of learning and living. You are going to forge a new path. To do that, you will need to be open to learning new skills and communication techniques, as well as to create new pathways in your brain, etc. It is going to be a process.

You will have to identify how you learn. Are you a reader? Do you learn better by listening to/watching a video or podcast? Do you learn more effectively 1:1? Do you understand better in a group setting? There are endless ways to learn with your counselor and on your own between sessions. The more work you put into this, the faster you will see results. And by faster, I mean in months instead of years. Improving our mindsets is something we actually should be working on daily throughout our lives. It's been said, "Work harder on yourself than you do in your career, marriage, friendships, business, etc." For anything in our lives to change, we need to change. Ouch! That hurts, doesn't it? The more you apply that sentence, the more empowering it will be to you. It goes back to what my friend

Patty taught her kids. When we own it, we can change it. And that, my friend, is how you do it. Own it.

Another critical step in healing our mindset is daily exercise. Stay with me here. Yes, I said daily exercise. How does that help our mindset and emotions? It helps every part of our body, down to every cell that makes up our body.

Let's review how exercise helps our mindset/emotions:

- As you exercise, you take deeper breaths, which leads to more oxygen in each cell. If your cells are well-oxygenated, that will help everything work better. How do you think that would make you feel if your body started to work better?
- When you exercise outside, you breathe fresh air and can take in the sights and sounds of nature. Does your mood improve after 30+ minutes of walking in your neighborhood, hiking at a local park, walking along a beach, or cycling on a scenic bike path?
- When you exercise, it gives your mind time to clear itself. Most people have some things they bring home from work, moments in their marriage or with their children, etc. As we exercise, our brains process these things and help us let them go if they are genuinely not urgent, or it works on coming up with a solution to the problem. Our time of exercise can be a creative windfall for us. I will be honest. I have been walking our dog for the last year, and many ideas for this book have come together as we walked. I don't use earbuds. I just walk. Whatever type of exercise you do, I encourage you to do some of it outside. Breathe in the fresh air and exhale the negativity running around in your mind.

Other options to help your mindset:

- Prayer/meditation. Quiet time spent alone with God. I know not all of you are believers. As you read this book, you can choose how you dedicate your quiet time. Quiet time with God can be silent, or it can be you, talking. But just as we pause to listen as another person talks in a real-life conversation, please wait to hear what God is saying to you. It isn't audible, but He talks to us sometimes by supplying us with a beautiful idea. It will come in a conversation with someone you know, and in so many other ways He can show you how to follow His will for your life.

- Write out or print out Bible verses or affirmations that confirm the new mindset you are working on. Say them aloud each day and throughout the day. Make a list of ten or so. I wouldn't suggest any more than that. You want the list short enough to learn and let your mind be able to embrace and work towards achieving.

- Create a music playlist. I created a playlist on YouTube of about six or so of my favorite worship songs. They meant a lot to me and touched my soul. Daily listening helped keep my focus on God, His power, His victory over death, and the devil's power. The more I listened to those songs, the deeper the meaning of each song would go in my mind. I didn't just know the words. I felt how God was moving in my body to heal me completely.

The process of healing your mindset and emotions is never linear. There are going to be ups and downs. There will be moments of doubt and feeling overwhelmed. Some steps you will have to take will be more challenging and cause you to learn more from the previous actions. But that is a good thing. The stronger your foundation is in the beginning, as you hit those more challenging steps in the middle and then again towards the pinnacle, you will be able to work through those levels of challenges that will be brought your way. Because you are strongest in the basics of mindset and emotion, as you rise, your strength will equip you to overcome significant challenges without as much angst.

A reminder that our Pastor, Kurt, shared one Sunday morning, "Don't use your words to describe your situation; use your words to change your situation."[4]

Steps to Healing Our Mindset and Emotions: Inventory Your Priorities

Not everyone has a firm grasp on a list of priorities numbered 1–7 in order of importance. If you do, you are a step further in the right direction for your life and health. If not, that is not a problem; you can work on it soon.

I want to share a few things I have learned along my life's path that may help you as you list out your priorities and fully understand what is meant by importance. People throw around what is essential to them today and next week. Something new is at the top of their life list of importance. That is not being real, authentic, and committed as you look at your life priorities.

I learned two crucial lessons in my life that helped me order priorities—one in my youth was growing up on the farm, and the other as a L/D nurse. If you have not lived on a farm, let me give you a little lesson on farm life. We do not have a strict schedule, per se. There is a schedule, but it is always subject to change depending on the weather and if the cows get out of their yards. We ate most of our meals together as a family because we all worked on the farm in one way or another. My dad had a "staff" meeting three times a day with my mom and us kids. Things may have changed from breakfast to dinner—on the farm, that is, our lunch meal; and by supper, our evening meal on the farm, plans for the evening could be more like what we had planned in the morning. This is how life goes with 300 head of cattle, a few barns full of pigs, and field corn/beans/hay in the fields.

Our dad had a firm handle on the business of our farm. He took a lot of things in stride and put total dependence on God for the provision of each day and season. However, as things came up, he would redirect our plans each day to ensure we accomplished the best we could, given the circumstances. He rarely panicked. That part still amazes me. The only thing that made him jump from the table was when the cows had broken a fence, and they were running all over our farm and then out into the road. This was a problem and an actual emergency. We lived on a black-top, country road that had a fair amount of traffic on it. That meant we, along with our dad, all jumped and went to our assumed positions to help round up the cattle. We all had been through this "drill" before and knew our jobs. As in the armed forces, we practiced enough drills to be ready at the drop of a hat for the real things. Our dad was a phenomenal teacher. Again, I want to emphasize that he lived life calmly unless there was an actual reason—life or death—to show signs of any angst. Full disclosure. I am still a work in progress in this area.

In nursing school, I worked as a nursing assistant in a high-risk antepartum unit at my University's Hospital. We had most of the state's "problem pregnancies" in our department. One Sunday afternoon, a patient had just returned from her allowed wheelchair ride to go outside and smoke. She put on her emergency light in the bathroom as she was bleeding A LOT. I will never forget the charge nurse and how she handled this true-life/death emergency. She peeked her head out of the patient room and calmly said, call L/D and tell them we will be bringing this patient on a gurney; and they should be ready to go to the OR. We all did our part. That patient was on a gurney, rolled quickly around the "corner" to L/D, leaving a trail of blood on the carpet from her room to her destination. The scene was bad. But we all remained calm because of the charge nurse's direction and tone of voice. The baby was born in the next few minutes via c-section, and all remained healthy.

I took a few key points from my dad and the many charge nurses I learned from. True emergencies happen in life. But not every problem is a life and death emergency. If life is not at stake, it may be urgent but not emergent. These mentors who taught me this critical difference made a significant impact as I practiced as a L/D nurse. A former colleague reminded me as we were putting our scrubs on one day, "Ann, as we put these on, we need to be ready for every OB situation." And she was right. I worked in hospitals with a larger L/D department, and we saw enough to know the difference between an emergency and someone who wasn't dealing well with pain during their labor. We provided each patient with excellent care, but only the true emergencies got the priority they well deserved.

Think about the priorities in your life and the order in which you place them. Please give some careful thought to the importance that you give them. That number one spot is something that you may have to die for. Keep that in mind when you write your priorities out. Are you willing to possibly give your life for it? I am not typing this to be melodramatic. As a parent, a family member, and a nurse, I have seen a lot and learned the value of our priorities in the proper order. It has provided us with stability and knowledge that we are on the same page, and we know by looking each other in the eye when we are in true emergency mode or if it is just an annoyance trying to impersonate an actual emergency.

What about your personality? I am just "wired" this way. Let's discuss how we are wired. I will refer to the birth order analogy as that is the simplest one to make my point concisely. There are the oldest children. We refer to them as "Type A" people—everything has a place, and there is a place for everything, type of person. There is the middle child—everything in their world must be fair. And then there is the youngest child—this one wants everything now and to be included in everything. Your personality has to meld with your priorities, no matter your type. Let me put it this way. In my last OB unit, we had about 150 nurses, all women. We had a spectrum of personalities, but we had the same order of priorities when it came to patient care. We all knew the order of importance, and we all knew our jobs in each given circumstance. We functioned like a well-oiled machine, making each patient feel as if they were the best. We had a fantastic team.

As we look at our priorities in the sense of a family, we each have different personalities. Still, we need to use each person's character strengths and "massage" our weaknesses to thrive in our lives and within our priorities. When we do this, our relationships and lives hum like a fine-tuned Porsche. And as we would with a fine-tuned Porsche, we need to work daily on both.

Let's get to work on taking inventory of our priorities. Here are some steps I have come up with and believe will give you a good running start. You, however, can add or tweak things that will provide you with a more straightforward look into your specific priorities.

Step 1: Go somewhere.

- Coffee shop
- Park
- Beach
- Lake cabin
- Beautiful resort; sit in their lobby, restaurant, or by the pool if that is an option for the day.
- Take a hike; find a vista that provides you with a calm spot to think.

Step 2: Bring an empty notebook and some writing utensils.

Step 3: Silence your phone and put it in your purse/bag/backpack.

Step 4: Clear out the mess in your mind by taking time to clear it before you start. Listen to a podcast or music, or just close your eyes and let your mind empty all of the daily clutter.

Step 5: Take out your notebook and write out the priorities people most commonly use. Do not assign them numbers, but leave some space between them to jot down some notes.

- Faith
- Family
- Career
- Health (mental/physical/nutrition)
- Vacation/Travel
- Financial
- Philanthropy

Take some time and write notes beside each priority.

- What is essential in each of them?
- Why is each of those items important?
- How does this priority play out in your life? Is it something you do/think about daily/weekly/yearly?

Do not hurry this step. Do some soul-searching. The process is not a race to get this done as quickly as possible. This is a thought-provoking exercise that should have you clarifying some areas of your life that you may have been avoiding and not giving the attention that you need. If you are married, here are a few ideas. You may want to do this separately and then discuss your findings together. In a marriage, ultimately in our marriage, we are one. In this process, we find out where we may be a bit off target; we may find where we clash, and hopefully, we can come together to build each other up and create a marriage that genuinely becomes in alignment in this area, too.

Step 6: Time to put them in order.

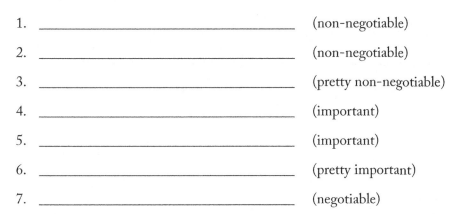

1. _____ (non-negotiable)

2. _____ (non-negotiable)

3. _____ (pretty non-negotiable)

4. _____ (important)

5. _____ (important)

6. _____ (pretty important)

7. _____ (negotiable)

You can change the words to the right, but I wanted to help you remember that this process is necessary. If you take this seriously, it can help you in all areas of your life. It can be a vital step to review the list with your counselor or mentor. It will help deepen your conversations and help them understand you more fully.

If they are not interested in this, may I suggest you start looking for a better person to help you completely heal mentally.

When you have completed this, take some time and then review it in a few days, and then again in another few days. If this resonates with you, or you and your spouse, after a week or two, commit it to the rest of your life. Your new list of priorities is your firm foundation, and it is how you make your decisions—all of them. Everything comes back to this. Everything. Your priorities remain the same regardless of how our culture shifts or changes. If the crowd jumped off the cliff, would you? Know the order and importance of your priorities and stand in them firmly.

Steps to Healing Our Mindset and Emotions: Clarifying Our Health Priorities

One of our priorities above is our health priority, which encompasses nutrition, exercise, and mental understanding of our health. Let's take a laser focus on this to help us clarify some things that will help us and, most likely, our families.

Why is this so important to understand deeply? Because although there seems to be a pill for everything now, they don't solve the root problem. The pills mask the symptoms for almost everything they are prescribed. Disclaimer: There are some pills and treatments some of us need, and there is no other way to have a better health outcome. For example, Type 1 Diabetics need insulin. High blood pressure because of a genetic predisposition may mean antihypertensives are necessary for your care plan. Currently, chemotherapy is the best course of action for my colon cancer. I want to help educate you and help you become an incredible advocate for your health and, if called to be, an outstanding advocate for your family or friend if asked.

Step 1: Describe your desires for your future health. We can't predict our future completely, but we can realize there are some things we can control and implement. A critical thought to keep in mind as you move forward is this: **What are you willing to change in your ranking of priorities to achieve your future health status?** You are not lowering your future health status to match your current priorities.

- It is NOT the number on the bathroom scale; don't even list it. The number on the scale is part of our overall health journey, and it is NOT THE GOAL. You know the weight that, when you stand in front of the mirror naked or with clothes on, you feel good about what you see.
- How do you want to feel?
- What do you want to be able to do? Activity for fun and activity for exercise?
- How do you see yourself living?
  - Describe the details of your desired health.
  - Contributions to your family/community because of your level of health.
  - Reverse or improve a chronic illness that you may have—Type 2 Diabetes, hypertension (non-genetic), correct cholesterol numbers, decrease BMI if >30.

Step 2: Prioritize your health priority list.

- Exercise
  - What are things you love to do for exercise?
  - What do you have available—home, outside, or gym/class?
  - What fits in your financial budget for your exercise?
  - Do you utilize technology to complement your exercise—app or web-based?
  - What amount of time do you have to exercise each day or week? Re-evaluate on a monthly or quarterly basis.

- Do you need a goal of 5K, 10K, half marathon, or marathon? Bike ride goal? Step goal for walking for the year (5 million steps in a year/14,100 each day)?
- What is your level of commitment to exercise? This detail will help you set your pace and your goals.

- Nutrition
  - How are you doing? Excellent, needs improvement, or bad?
  - What information do you need to make better choices?
  - What is your budget for your nutrition?
  - Do you have a good amount of recipes?
  - Do you need more recipes or meal plan ideas?
  - Do you need more help to learn how to cook better?
  - Do you have a garden, or is it possible to have one?
  - Do you have access to fresh meat/fish/chicken? (My naturopath encouraged me to get to know my farmer.)
  - What is your level of commitment to making changes in your food choices? Knowing this will help you set your pace and your goals.

- Handling and mitigating stress
  - How do you currently manage when a stressful event happens in your life?
  - Is everything terrible that happens considered an "emergency" even if it is not life-threatening?
  - Do you alter your health goals because of a problem in another area of your life that came up unexpectedly but is not a true emergency?
  - Do you alter some of your top priorities because of unexpected problems each time they arise?
  - Have you asked or thought of asking for help with how you manage when stressful events happen?

- How would your life change if you could learn new techniques or ideas to help you mitigate how you react to more minor or mid-level stress events?
- Are you ready to commit to learning new things and unlearning old habits that do not serve you?

- Comprehensive team for your health (this is like a menu, think a la cart)
  - Primary Care Physician
  - Focused Area Physician—Cardiologist, Oncologist, etc.
  - Pyschiatrist, Psychologist, Counselor, etc.
  - Naturopathic Physician
  - Functional Medicine Physician
  - Chiropractor
  - Massage Therapist
  - Dietician
  - Acupuncturist

- Preventive care
  - Are you current with your preventive care appointments?
    - Routine lab work—cholesterol/lipid panel, blood sugar & HgbA1C, and CBC
    - Yearly physical which assesses you, head to toe
    - Dermatology
    - Mammograms for women >/= 40 years old who have breasts
    - Testicular and Prostate exams for men
    - Colonoscopy at 45 years old, as of 2021, or per your family history & risk factors

- Do you have habits not recommended by research that are detrimental to your health?
  - Smoking
  - Recreational and illegal drugs

- Drink too much alcohol
- Not exercising at all and capable of
- Unhealthy eating habits—binging, bulimia, or anorexia
- Multiple or many sex partners

- Make a plan for your pace of change.

  - Is your health at a point where you have a diagnosis or two of chronic disease(s) that you need to make more changes quickly?
  - Is your health showing signs of numbers creeping outside of "normal limits," and you can make changes at a moderate pace?
  - Is your health "within normal limits," and changes are genuinely up to you for the pace that you want to make changes?

Replicate the process that you did for the overall life priorities. Rate what is most important within your health, from Emergent or Urgent to "would be important," to start working on at a steady pace. This will be different for everyone; and as a married couple, this will most likely bring on a vibrant conversation with your spouse. Art and I have had many. He is such a good sport and partner in our health journey.

One more step to add at the bottom of both lists:

- Obstacles

  - Learn to ask me—How can I? Instead of the innate response of feeling/being overwhelmed and the actions that follow the latter response.
  - If _____ happens, I am going to do _____.
  - If this choice in my food plan is not available, I will look for options B, C, or D as the next healthier option. You will not veer off track quickly or as far if you have a plan.

- I like to run outside. What is your commitment for rain, snow, or temperatures <40 degrees Fahrenheit? A plan B or C for exercise in inclement weather will keep you on track for each season of the year.
- What will I do in an actual emergency or stressful situations for each area?
  ○ How many meals are justifiable for me to slide in an emergent situation/stressful situation?
  ○ How many days am I ok with missing exercising for when an emergency happens?
- Birthdays—outside of your immediate family—extended family relatives, coworkers, neighbors, etc. Are they a priority to celebrate? We can't celebrate and go off plan for EVERY person's birthday. It doesn't mean that you are rude and say that you can't participate; but take some time to make a plan about whose birthdays you will celebrate full out, those that you will have a bit of a cheat on, and those that you will just wish them well, and not feel guilty for not participating.

- But my family is not on board.

  - Are you thoroughly committed to the changes you want to make?
  - Have you had an honest and open conversation with them?
  - Have you made a few new recipes for them before letting them shut you down?
  - Have you sat down to discuss a change of plan everyone can agree on? Each family member can have some variations in the speed of pace. This is not a dictatorship. This is learning to lead by example and adding finesse and creativity to get the family on board.

You have created both lists—the more general priority list and your health list can be much more focused. For any other part of your lists on which you want to get more specific, please search out authors or mentors in those subject areas. They are available and will work with you. Or, if you read their books or listen to their podcasts, you will hear their advice and be able to implement their strategies from there.

This chapter has a lot in it. This chapter covers the area most people don't work on when looking at their health goals. They generally think about food and exercise. That is why most people say, "I know what to do. I just don't do it." Let me translate that for you. People, in general, know the facts. They don't fully know WHY they want to change, nor do they desire the NEED to make the changes. The WHY is in our mindset. If we don't change our mindset by unlearning wrong information and learning new credible information, we won't make the changes long term. Also, we have to know the other part of our WHY—our emotional reason why we will make these changes and not return to our old habits. Spend time on this chapter. Make the time to do some "soul searching." It is worth it. You will change the direction of your life and health. You will inspire your family and those close to you. You may inspire more than you know. How do I know you will inspire others? Others are watching. Anytime we make changes and results are visible or tangible, people take notice. Others that know us well or watch us from "the periphery" of our relationships are wondering if "it" works. And when they see that you are making lifestyle changes that do work long term, they start building their confidence to make similar changes. You may not have thought about it, and maybe you don't want this "responsibility." But it is not your "responsibility." You are shining a light towards someone else in their dark struggles and providing them enough light to take the first step on their journey. That may be a little too deep. But it is true.

Today, work on one thing. Tomorrow, work on it a little bit more. The next day, continue the work. You are creating a new routine one day at a time. The questions listed above will help you figure out precisely what is the best first step for you. Take it.

There are no questions to journal at the end of this chapter because of all of the questions within the chapter. When you are ready, let's learn more things that you can do to support a healthier life.

SEEDS SOWN

CHAPTER 12

RESTORATION IN
FUELING OUR BODIES

"Daniel then said to the guard who the chief official had appointed over
Daniel, Hannaniah, Mishael and Azariah, 'Please test your servants
for ten days: Give us nothing but vegetables to eat and water to drink.
Then compare our appearance with that of the young men who eat the
royal food, and treat your servants in accordance with what you see.'
So he agreed to this and tested them for ten days. At the end of the ten
days they looked healthier and better nourished than any of the young
men who ate the royal food. So the guard took away their choice food
and the wine they were to drink and gave them vegetables instead."

DANIEL 1:11-16 NIV

Shortly after my colon polyp diagnosis, I started forming my team. I had the
apparent players—a surgeon and an oncology referral, friends in the oncology
field, and a massage therapist. But I knew I needed more. To me, a team meant

holistic. I wanted my team to include all modalities. I tried to fight this disease with all hands on deck. I was not going down without a whole team fighting on my behalf. I am well aware that nutrition fuels our bodies, and the information is vast in this area. I wanted a person who had wisdom in nutrition and the medical impact it can have on our bodies. I knew of someone, but I wasn't near her. Tanda is a naturopathic doc. I followed her on social media and listened to the information that she shared. Her knowledge is research based. I aligned with her philosophy because it is credible. The only access to her that I had was a message through Facebook. Would she read my message? Would she be willing to take me on as a patient? We weren't in close proximity. If she agreed, how was this going to work?

I stopped asking questions and sent the message. Tanda replied. She wanted to talk with me without strings attached. I was blown away by her compassion. We exchanged phone numbers and set a time to speak.

I programmed Tanda's number into my cell phone, and I was ready with pen and paper when she called. I can best describe her philosophy by looking at everything nutrition, supplements, exercise, mental, medical, etc. She looks broader and more in depth at our whole lives as she cares for her patients. I decided she would be the perfect complement to the medical care I wanted to use. I took copious notes because I needed to be able to explain her plan to my husband. Art listened and digested all of the information; he was intrigued, and in the end, on board.

I informed Tanda of our decision and that I wanted to be her patient. She shared how her practice works, the cadence of our appointments, and the resources she would share with me. Establishing new care with a new provider can be a tad overwhelming. Tanda creates a culture of calm with each of her patients. She also shares in an easy-to-learn way the wisdom she has accumulated through her years of practice. She coaches her patients, which is unique to her practice. Her goal is that her patients apply what she shares, not just let the information go in one ear and then out the other.

When I made this decision, I knew the amount of learning that would occur in my life during my treatment was going to be exponential. I was going to learn more about surgery, colon cancer treatment, and a wide variety of learning from Tanda. I was all in. I wanted to know everything I could in all these areas and more. If there was information that would help me, I would access it and learn it. I did have to filter everything through my nursing knowledge, though. Some things that I read were not sound in their foundation, and I would put them aside. With each piece of information I read, I learned more; and it helped equip me with every new decision I needed to make for my care plan.

As I have shared earlier in this book, I have been studying more about nutrition for many years. I learned about Tanda at a business conference. From that point, I followed her through groups centered on nutrition and "friended" her on Facebook. Social media posts are an option for all to learn from her.

Now, as her patient, I was given up close and personal access to her knowledge and the specific plan she came up with for me to follow. This plan would go alongside my medical plan. I informed my medical team, and they were receptive to Tanda's plan. Why? Because her philosophy is solid and wicked smart.

What did I learn from Tanda, and how did the implementation go?

Here is most of my list:

- Follow a paleo eating plan for 90 days straight.
  - I was able to follow it from early March until I started chemotherapy in late April. When I started having nausea from the chemotherapy, I reverted to some more bland things and some choices that were not fully paleo. I didn't entirely go off track, but I could not complete 90 days of paleo. I had to have some nutrients that stayed down and fueled my body.
- Source your food carefully. Tanda's philosophy is to "know your farmer." Her recommendations are to shop for your food locally. If you can, get to know who grows your food—eggs, meat, vegetables, and fruit.

- Grow your food. Tanda is a proponent of growing your food if you are able. I was honest with her, and she agreed that starting to be an avid vegetable gardener may not be my focus during my treatment. I did start doing research and learning how to be a Florida gardener.

- Remove gluten. I implemented that 90%. After I finished treatment, I discovered that I had been diagnosed with Celiac. I am 100% gluten-free now.

- No processed foods for 90 days straight. I cried. I knew the products I represented were good for my body, but I stopped using them for 90+ days.

- She supplied me with supplements that would help my body during treatment. This point is essential to note, and please consult your doctor(s) before taking any supplements. Your doctor can tell you which ones will be safe and not interact with your meds, treatments, or other supplements.

- She encouraged me at night to apply externally to my liver a nickel's amount of organic castor oil, using my fingers, and to sleep in a cotton t-shirt. You also can make "castor oil packs."

- Tanda educated me on the importance of "dry brushing" to aid in the movement of my lymph system.

- Vitamin D absorption from sunlight. My instructions were to sit out on our patio for 10–15 minutes in a sleeveless shirt and shorts. I was instructed not to apply sunscreen to my skin for this part of her plan. I routinely wear sunscreen to help me prevent my risk of skin cancer. I see my dermatologist yearly.

- Drink water. Stay hydrated. No caffeine.

- Sleep 7–8 hours or more each night, as needed.

- Stress. We talked a lot about this topic since she knew what was happening in our personal lives besides my medical diagnosis.

- Exercise. Tanda was pleased with my consistent walking and encouraged me to continue. I was encouraged to do whatever I wanted if any other movement was tolerable.
- Take 100 deep breaths every day. Oxygenation of our cells is vital for overall health.
- Meditation and prayer.
- Have fun. Live with JOY. Play. These phrases are part of Tanda's core philosophies. And she ensures her patients understand how important this is in our lives.

We met consistently over the phone. Tanda educated me, monitored my progress, and guided me through my treatment. Her care was impactful on many levels. She filled in the gaps not covered in our routine medical care team. She talked with me about subjects I would have had to connect with multiple traditional practitioners, taking more time and fragmenting my care. I want to clarify a fine point: I added Tanda to complement the high level of traditional medical care I was receiving. I didn't add her because my medical care was subpar. Each doctor has their specialty, and all of mine are excellent. Tanda's specialty is holistic, natural medical care. She delivered up and above what I expected.

You may be reviewing the list above and saying, "But Ann, this isn't ground-breaking information. It is going back to the basics." Tanda reinforced what we have gotten away from because food-like substances in boxes and bags easily tempt us. We think eating real whole food is depriving! Think about this?! I was in that circle of temptation for a chunk of my life. I caved in to the desire and "addiction" to processed foods. And it took me a long time to get them out of my life. I still will have something processed occasionally, which is the keyword. I rarely eat processed foods, i.e., macaroni and cheese, frozen GF pizza, etc.

I cook from scratch for about 90+% of our meals.

Nutrition During My Treatment

I have shared what I did to prepare with Tanda before my surgery. I dialed in my nutrition to only a paleo food plan. My primary goal was to fuel my body for surgery, the recovery and to be prepared for the chemotherapy IF I was diagnosed with cancer, which I was. With this plan, I was eating whole foods and focused on eating a wide variety of colors of vegetables and fruits to provide the most comprehensive amount of nutrients possible. I took the prescribed supplements, including pre/probiotics. My surgeon had ordered a CT scan before surgery to confirm that there was only a polyp in my colon and nothing that would surprise him. That test confirmed there was only one polyp. That was a massive relief for me.

After surgery, a few things were apparent. I had lost 25 lb. I am 5' 4" tall, and I stepped on the scale one morning a few weeks after my surgery and gasped! It read 115 lb. My weight was not good. I consulted with Tanda, and we continued with our plan. She knew the resilience of our bodies after going through stress. I was concerned, but I also trusted Tanda. I continued with my Paleo eating choices.

My sister, Susie, was concerned; and I agreed with her. I started taking a picture of each of my meals and texting that picture to her. I wanted her to know I was eating a good meal three times a day. At this point, my diagnosis was not public knowledge. I had to be very careful with my pictures on social media.

I will never forget two days as I approached my chemo treatment. I needed a "port a cath" placed into my subclavian vein for chemotherapy treatment—another trip to the OR. The night before my surgery, I called my sister in a panic. I had just showered and caught sight of myself in the mirror. I looked gaunt and sickly. The nurse, who is not a good patient, started overthinking the situation. I had significant body image thoughts going through my mind. I remembered that the OR crew had to "paint" my chest to sterilize the area where my surgeon surgically implanted the port. I looked at what was left of my chest at this weight and cried.

I knew they weren't going to be shocked at what they saw. But I was. I knew I had to keep my nutrition in focus every day. I knew God was totally in control, but I knew I had to do my part with what I consumed.

The other day was the first day of chemotherapy. Our country and the world were still in COVID. During COVID, there were no visitors allowed for chemotherapy treatment. I had to go alone. I wasn't sure how I would feel after, so my daughter volunteered to be my driver. As I hopped out of the car, I asked her to take a picture of me. I knew I would share my story, and this picture would need to be documented in the right spot. When I looked at that picture, I was sickened. I had no hips. Before, my daughter would always kindly remind me, "Mom. You had three kids. You have earned the hips you have." And she was right. I had come to appreciate the body's shape God had given to me. And now it was gone.

I went into the Oncology center alone for my first chemo treatment. The first time you do anything, it is intimidating. Going in to have chemotherapy by yourself should never happen to anyone again. I had a personal pity party, put on my "big girl panties" and my mask, and walked up to the admitting gals with "Godfidence."

I soon learned the routine. My labs were drawn first. Next, I would talk with the NP. The last step was to go to the infusion room. Let me say this. I LOVE MY ONCOLOGY TEAM! The lab girls wore the biggest smiles that you could see behind those dang masks. They loved each of us as we started our day with this team. We hugged a lot! They were a chatty group and made the transition into a not-fun routine, a welcome relief.

The next stop was to see my Nurse Practitioner (NP). In this practice, you see the oncologist at the first visit and not until you finish treatment. I understood and soon learned that Heather, my NP, would be a prominent advocate for my care. From our first interaction, I knew she was sharp, caring, and open to answering all of my questions. I had a list of new questions and thoughts at each visit. She always had time to have great discussions with me. I will forever be thankful to Heather and the care she continues to give me.

The next part was the scariest to me—the infusion room. I had taken a tour on my first visit, but today was the real deal. It was time to start my chemotherapy treatment, so I found a recliner. It became "my" recliner. I sat in the same spot every time.

As I sat in my recliner, I immediately started assessing the staff. I saw the nurses working together and uniquely loving patients. Sherry was my nurse on the first day. She loved big! They know each patient is scared on the first day. They know we have a million questions on the first day. And they delivered a level of care that allowed me to exhale and start to relax. Sherry went through every detail about the routine, the meds, the timing, and the details of what I may experience. It was a lot to take in. But she held my hand and said it would be all good. And she was right.

When she went to the right side to access my port, I said, "It's on my left side." She was surprised, asked who my surgeon was, and paused. A short discussion took place. She accessed my port and got good blood flow. She smiled. I was relieved. And from her body language, I got it. My port was all good.

I wasn't sure how I would feel, so I brought a book to read, my computer to work on, and headphones to listen to music. As you can guess, I ended up talking with my sister after settling in. She wanted to know every detail I learned and how I felt as this treatment started. Thankfully, my recliner was in a corner, so my phone conversation wasn't interrupting anyone else.

The infusion team works together—the nurses "tag-team" the patients in the room. So, I got to know each of the staff pretty quickly. I soon learned that Julie was the head nurse. She loved everyone who walked in the door and knew each by name. She also knew them—she greeted them and asked personal questions; she knew what to ask to make them feel comfortable as they walked in each day of their treatment.

At one point on my first day, Julie came to meet and get to know me. Before she left me, she looked at me; and we locked eyes. She said,

---

"No one wants to be part of this family. But if you have to be part of this family, we are the family you want."

I smiled, I cried, and we hugged. I am still crying as I type this paragraph. She nailed it. No one wants cancer. No one wants a treatment that will make them feel like crap. No one wants to sit in the infusion room alone. But I soon learned I was never alone again as I walked into each infusion day. I had a new family. I was part of the oncology family, and they had adopted me. And we were going to create a lot of memories together. From that point on, I had a new attitude. And some days, as I walked in, I didn't think they knew what to do with me. I walked in with a smile that didn't stop, and I hugged everyone as I entered the room.

I bought a pair of red tennis shoes to wear for each day of my chemo treatment. And I did wear them the first couple weeks, but then I started to make a switch. I began wearing stilettos. I always dressed nicely, but I started making a point to pick out an outfit that would add class to the infusion center. As my sister's mother-in-law, Millie says when I walk into their house, "Ann, you always add a little sparkle when you arrive." And so, I added some "sparkle" to the infusion center every other Monday. Game on.

My chemo treatment went like this. Monday morning was a 3–4 hour time of infusion. I was given medications to decrease nausea first. Then came the chemotherapy combo. Before I left, they would give me a cassette of the last chemo drug and titrate the infusion to a low level, then infuse it for 48 hours. I didn't mind bringing home the infusion until I went to bed that first night. The cassette made a noise every 30 seconds to push the medication through the tubing. Not good. I needed quality sleep. It took me a few nights to figure out how to wrap the cassette in towels to muffle the noise. I would return on Wednesday mornings to have it stopped, and IV setup discontinued.

The first round of chemo was not bad. I had to push back the 2nd round of chemo because of the change in insurance we experienced. When I had the 3rd infusion, I started to feel the side effects of the chemo. The side effects of chemo were my new "normal." During the week of chemo, I felt as if I were nine weeks pregnant. Nausea. The nausea wasn't horrible, but nausea is still never good. I also started feeling exhausted on Wednesday afternoon and going into Thursday. The week after chemo was better.

Let's talk nutrition and feeling nauseated. It's a short discussion. When you are nauseated, not much sounds good. I am thankful that I never threw up as a result of the anti-nausea drugs they gave me on Monday. I was just mildly-mediumly nauseated Wednesday–Saturday, and then it would taper off. That's when I decided I would have to make a new plan. I wouldn't be able to stay on a strict paleo diet. Paleo means no grains. I had to include some bland foods to get me through nausea and not lose any weight. I was maintaining my weight at 115 lb, but I knew it could go down if I wasn't careful.

I talked with Tanda, and she supported my decision. She knew it would have been better to stay on the Paleo plan for 90 days straight, but she also listened to how I was feeling and tried to stay as close to Paleo as possible. I made some reasonable substitutions that would give me nutrients but be blander to keep my nausea at its lowest point and still allow me to eat. I found a happy medium, and things continued to be stable. Ironically, after COVID, my weight shifted, and I started to gain weight. I gained 10–15 lb and remain steady at about 130 lb! Woot!

One of the things I was hesitant to use when I was not strictly adhering to Paleo was the nutrition products from the company I was affiliated with. Why? I was nauseated. I wanted to protect my favorite foods during that time. I didn't want a negative association with them. I decided on a week I felt good to try my morning "green" drink. This cocktail was a mix of powdered greens, a pre/probiotic with digestive enzymes, and a little thing we call a "fizz stick." I started adding it in more consistently after I had tolerated it a few mornings during my good week. I realized that this drink was adding nutrition to my body each day. No matter how I felt the rest of the day, I was getting a rainbow of nutrients at the start of each day. That was a huge win for my course. And no matter what else I could eat the rest of the day, I knew this morning "cocktail" was doing its thing each morning that I consumed it.

A few things to note: God blessed me to have stable labs through my entire treatment. I never had to have therapy delayed because my bloodwork was off. My care team was always impressed with that. I also believe that working with Tanda to focus on my nutrient-dense food choices helped.

Nutrition Really Is Basic

We need to eat the basics. We need to eat real food. Real food has everything we need to be the healthiest and provide our bodies with fuel to add to each cell's strength. It is this simple.

Unfortunately, we have been led astray over the years by the advertisers of processed foods and the mixed messages from scientific and medical communities. We have had to become diligent at verifying reliable sources and cross-checking research articles or authorities. As a society, we are so off course that it will feel like I suggest that we each go back a few hundred years in history with our eating choices. How archaic, right?! It may not seem reasonable or fair. Eating real food will primarily create a shift in all areas of your body and how you feel; and the numbers in your blood work will improve.

Calories. I don't talk about calories. Why? Eating a whole foods diet focuses on nutrients which are essential. Counting calories is overall useless. What?! Yes. Let's make a comparison. What is healthier—eating 2000 calories of processed foods or eating three meals of whole foods, primarily vegetables? The latter. No questions asked. Toss out the bags and the boxes in your pantry today. Here is a link to print out a picture of what your plate should look like at each meal. The Harvard Myplate is accurate.

Refer to it by visiting: https://www.hsph.harvard.edu/nutritionsource/healthy-eating-plate-vs-usda-myplate/

There are a lot of "names" of eating plan styles floating around out there. As I shared, I was encouraged to eat "Paleo." Paleo is essentially eating meat proteins, vegetables, fruit occasionally, most nuts, minimal natural sweeteners, and healthy fats. No grains, no dairy, no gluten, no added sugar, no legumes, no processed foods, and no caffeine. We are going to just talk about whole foods. Things that come out of the dirt, off of a tree or plant, and from an animal.

Focused Learning Leads to Implementation

To be licensed as a nurse, I attend Continuing Education Courses to stay up to date on my education. This past year, I participated in an Institute for Brain Potential class titled "An Anti-Inflammatory Lifestyle." This one-day class confirmed everything I had learned about nutrition in the past 15 years. All of the information in the course was cited and well researched.

I have read books, attended conferences, listened to many podcasts, and was attentive in any conversation that pertained to nutrition/health/wellness. In this section, I will summarize what I have learned throughout the years and share a few tips from this course.

Vegetables

Let's focus on the number of vegetables that we should consume daily. We must eat at least 7–9 servings of non-starchy vegetables daily. That is three servings of non-starchy vegetables at every meal each day. It's simple. These are the facts. They won't change your mind, so let's move on to the information that will.

- Vegetables are full of insoluble fiber, and this feeds gut bacteria. One hundred trillion bacteria will ferment the food in the colon. [1]
- The fiber in the vegetables promotes GI motility and a healthy GI tract. Daily bowel movements are a sign of health.
- We improve our system by eating cruciferous vegetables, increasing our body's ability to detoxify more effectively. [2]
  - Broccoli, cauliflower, Brussels sprouts, cabbage, kale, etc
- 10–50% of vegetables/plants are protein. Not enough protein in fruit only. [3]
- Plant protein does not turn on the aging factor. [4]
- The goal is to eat 30–40 DIFFERENT fruits and vegetables each week.
- Vegetables come in many colors. Eat all of the colors to have a wide variety of nutrients fuel your body.

Fruit

Fruit are brightly colored and full of antioxidants, vitamins, soluble fiber, and naturally occurring sugar.

- Soluble fiber found in fruit helps lower our LDL and non-HDL (cholesterol).
- Research varies in amount per day. 3–4 servings/week to 3 servings/day.
- During the digestion of whole fruit, the soluble fiber slows down the release of sugar into the bloodstream. So, we don't experience a quick spike in blood sugar when we eat the whole fruit. The fiber is gone when we drink fruit juice, and our blood sugar increases quickly during digestion.

Legumes

- Beans and legumes contain antioxidants that help prevent cell damage and fight disease and aging. The fiber and other nutrients benefit the digestive system, and may even help to prevent digestive cancers. [5]
- Types of legumes
  - Adzuki beans (also known as field peas or red beans): Soups, sweet bean paste, and Japanese and Chinese dishes
  - Anasazi beans: Soups and Southwestern dishes; can be used in recipes that call for pinto beans
  - Black-eyed peas (also known as cowpeas): Salads, casseroles, fritters, and Southern dishes
  - Edamame (also known as soybeans): Snacks, salads, casseroles, and rice dishes
  - Fava beans (also known as broad beans): Stews and side dishes
  - Garbanzo beans (also known as chickpeas): Casseroles, hummus, minestrone soup, and Spanish and Indian dishes
  - Lentils: Soups, stews, salads, side dishes, and Indian dishes
  - Soy nuts: Snack or garnish for salads [6]
  - Legumes contain large amounts of soluble fiber, protein, carbohydrates, B vitamins, iron, copper, magnesium, manganese, zinc, and phosphorus. Legumes are naturally low in fat, are practically free of saturated fat; and because they are plant foods, they are cholesterol-free as well. Along with being a highly nutritious food, evidence shows that legumes can play an important role in the prevention and management of a number of health conditions. [7]
  - All legumes, when served with a grain, contain all the essential amino acids and are recommended as protein choices, especially for vegetarians or vegans. [8]

Meat

Meats are not shown per current research in 2019 to reduce mortality. Read that again. According to the American Heart Association, plant-based and Mediterranean diets, along with increased fruit, nut, vegetable, legume, and lean vegetable or animal protein (preferably fish) consumption, with the inherent soluble and insoluble vegetable fiber, have consistently been associated with lower risk of all-cause mortality than control or standard diets. [9]

- "We can eat animal protein for the taste or just because we want to. We can no longer say that we eat animal protein for our health." [10]
- Animal protein turns on inflammation and pathways, increasing cancer growth and insulin resistance. Plant protein does not turn on the aging pathway. [11]
- Ocean-caught seafood has been shown to lower the risk of mortality.
- My naturopath, Tanda, recommends eating grass-fed, pasture-raised meat and eggs. The omega-6s in this type of meat are lower and have higher levels of nutrients than conventionally raised meat.

Healthy Fats

Healthy fats are just that; they are healthy. They benefit your health, and you want to eat them EVERY DAY.

- Healthy fats help us stay full longer.
- Healthy fats help our HDL; the healthy cholesterol number maintains or increases it. The optimal level for HDL is >60.
- Healthy fats are high in Omega-3.
    - Fish—Salmon, tuna, mackerel, anchovies, sardines, striped bass (fish from the ocean, not from a "fish farm")
    - Nuts—Walnuts, almonds, hazelnuts
    - Seeds—Flaxseed, Chia Seeds, Pumpkin Seeds
    - Avocados

Fermented Foods

- Fermented foods provide your body with beneficial probiotics. Probiotics help seed your microbiome with beneficial bacteria.
- Sources—Kefir, sauerkraut, kombucha, miso, kimchi, apple cider vinegar
- Horseradish is not fermented but is rich in antioxidants.

Sugar

- The average American consumes 82 gm/day of sugar.
- Added sugars contribute to cardiovascular disease, the world's number one cause of death. In fact, a 2014 study found that people who consumed 17–21 percent of their calories from added sugars had a 38 percent higher risk of dying from cardiovascular disease than people who got 8 percent of their calories from added sugar.
- Eating a diet high in added sugar can also increase the risk of diabetes, high blood pressure, unhealthy cholesterol levels, obesity and more. [12]
- The American Heart Association recommends that women have </=25 grams of added sugar/day and men have </= 36 grams of added sugar/ day.
  - Tip: track your processed sugar for one week on a sheet of paper. Tally up the grams of sugar each day. How many grams of added sugar are you consuming each day? Did it surprise you? If you are above 30 gm/day, make a plan SOON to start reducing the grams of sugar/day until you are at or below 25 gm/day if you are a woman. This needs to be high on your nutrition priority list.
- We should avoid artificial sweeteners. They are processed and not natural.
- Sugar in fruits or milk is NOT processed sugar.
- Sources of PROCESSED SUGAR
  - White and Brown sugar
  - Honey

- Malt Sugar
- Corn Syrup
- High Fructose Corn Syrup
- Invert Sugar
- Fruit Juice Concentrates
- Raw Sugar
- Syrup
- Molasses
- All sugar molecules ending in "ose" like dextrose, fructose, glucose, lactose, maltose, and sucrose [13]

Results of Eating Real Food

When we consume whole foods, we will notice one or more of the following changes in our bodies:

- Decreased inflammation
- Our filter organs—lungs, liver, kidneys, skin, and colon—work more efficiently.
- Decreased chronic illnesses
- Improved cholesterol, blood sugar, BMI, and BP numbers
- Increased energy, better sleep, less bloating, to name a few
- Clearer skin
- Adding nutrients that are easily absorbed

We all have a choice to make as we learn new information. Will we unlearn the things that do not serve us or statements that have been disproven by recent and more comprehensive research studies? Are we going to embrace the new information? Do we need to find further resources to help us embrace the latest research results? What is "winning" in your mind now—emotions or facts?

This list aims to help you learn more and shore up the things you know. Most items in our nutrition history have not changed. Some things have shifted because of mass production and adding processed food-like products that have overtaken our grocery stores. Most of these food-like, processed products do not have research on how they improve our health.

We have credible scientific research that we can review. There is updated research and still others that are not credible or long-term. I am working very hard with the information I share to focus on credible and long-term research. I also am trying to keep it simple for you to implement—real whole foods.

When we eat real whole foods and take out everything that is "food-like," it gives our body the ability to correct its core problems. This plan does not mask symptoms. It heals the body by decreasing inflammation, the core problem of most chronic diseases. It heals because it is a plan you implement long-term. Let me give you this example. What do you put into your car gas tank—gas, water, oil, soda? Simple, you put gas in your car. You would never think of putting anything in your gas tank except gas because you know it would immediately ruin your engine. The problem we have as we eat "food-like" products is that we do not have an immediate impact. We don't pay the price for our poor food choices until years later. And that's how our emotions get in the middle of this discussion. We are "addicted" to processed "food-like" products: the sugar, salt, and fat trifecta fuel our addiction. And our mind LOVES the "high" we get when we consume them. That is why it is a hard circle to break.

Implementing a "New" Nutrition Plan into Your Life

I have just provided some more facts and research about whole food to help provide clarity for you. Next, let's consider the timing of your eating. More research has looked into the times throughout the day optimal for us to eat and provide time for our bodies to rest. Some patterns help our bodies function optimally and then work best over the whole of our life span.

The plans centered on fasting are well researched. It is essential to take time to clarify a few points about fasting. Let's go back to the typical American eating pattern. We eat from the time we wake up until we go to sleep. We consume food daily as if we are at a buffet. We eat our meals, nibble, and snack between meals and after dinner. This pattern makes our pancreas, which secretes the insulin to regulate blood sugar, work non-stop until we cease eating as we go to bed. The pancreas is not designed to work that hard. What is optimal?

The current term for this is fasting. Let me clarify. Fasting can look like a "normal" pattern to eat and also a few variations depending on how you want to personalize it. The philosophy behind this is that it puts breaks between your eating—no more buffet style of eating from rising to bedtime. And the research is available to share the results.

Types of fasting:

- You are eating breakfast, lunch, and dinner. There are no snacks between meals and no eating after dinner. That provides your pancreas with 4–5 hours of rest between each meal and about 12 hours overnight.
- Eating from 11 am–7 pm. That is 8 hours of eating and 18 hours of no eating. That gives your pancreas a longer time frame at night to rest and not work.
- The eating window can vary per person, but generally is eating from 6–12 hours each day and fasting from 12–18 hours overnight. Each person can utilize the time frame that works for them.

*For more research on fasting, reference the book by Dr. Fung, "The Obesity Code," and the research located on www.pubmed.gov.

*Before changing your eating habits, please consult your PCP or other doctors providing your care to confirm these changes will be appropriate for you.

What happens when we fast for at least 12 hours? There are multiple benefits and also high patient adherence to these fasting patterns.

- Improves circadian rhythms

- Improves quality of life
- Improves sleep satisfaction
- Decreases hunger
- Decreases oxidative stress
- Decreases inflammation
- Decreases atherosclerosis
- Improves the gut microbiome
- Decreases blood pressure
- Decreases body weight
- Decreases body fat
- Increases glycemic control
- Increases glucose tolerance
- Decreases insulin resistance
- Decreases cholesterol numbers [14]

The list shows excellent results. I hope this information is giving you pause to think and then make some changes that would be best for you. Bringing credible research to your providers will be a welcome point of discussion for you and your doctor. After a thorough discussion, you will then be able to make the best decision.

I am continuing to tweak and improve my eating routine on an ongoing basis. After reading the research and changing things over the years, what have I settled on?

- Diagnosed with Celiac: I am gluten free.
- Plant-rich—the goal is to have most meals with 3+ servings of vegetables
- Fruits—1–2 servings/day
- Meat—ocean-caught seafood, organic chicken, eggs, grass-fed bison, and some occasional bacon, sausage, and steak
- Daily kombucha

- Greens "cocktail" each morning
- 80–100 oz of water/day
- Green tea
- Vegan protein shake for breakfast (4 gms of sugar)
- Minimal dairy/cheese
- Black/Pinto/White/Kidney beans, dry
- Added sugar +/- 25gms/day (my goal is <25 gms, but if I have a few extra grams occasionally, I call that good.)
- Rarely having peanuts (1–2 times/year)

I am hungry in the morning, through the early afternoon and less hungry in the evening. I eat from 7 am–7 pm most days. My goal is to have 12–14 hours of fasting overnight. Some days fall outside those times, and it turns out it is ok. I have a strong awareness but no hyper-focus or obsession around the timing. That is the full effect of creating healthy habits—they don't consume you. They become part of you. Through education, application, and seeing the results, your choices become second nature; and the temptations that previously drew you off course fade away like rain evaporating as the sun comes out after a storm.

The significant part of being on this healthy path is that, when you have celebrations, you can enjoy them. Going "off-plan" and enjoying a "vacation meal" is okay. Because they are occasional and no longer daily, you don't miss out. You are in charge of choosing the events that are important to you to enjoy. It is true "balance." And these celebrations don't impact your health because they are so sporadic that your body can quickly and easily flush out the "extras." Your body runs so well now that you don't experience the ups and downs on the scale.

I am not a chef or a creator of recipes, but I wanted to share our FAVORITE soup recipe. We make it at least once a month because it is tasty and nutritious. I credit my Marine Corps Momma friend, Heather, who graciously shared it with me after sharing a picture and review of it on social media. And a special mention goes to the original creator, Kylee. She is a recent culinary graduate.

There is something in a homemade chicken soup that is healing. And the addition of the combinations of vegetables and spice choices Kylee has combined makes it uber-healthy. Her blog is www.kyleeskitchenblog.com. It has ALL THE NUTRIENTS. Enjoy this recipe as it will become a family favorite of yours too!

Kylee's Kitchen Flu-Fighting Soup [15]

Yield: Makes about 10, 1-cup servings

Ingredients

- 2 Tablespoons coconut oil
- 1 1/2 cups carrots (about 2 large), medium dice
- 1 cup red pepper (about 1 large), medium dice
- 1/2 teaspoon salt (more to taste)
- 1/2 cup white button or cremini mushrooms, sliced
- 6 green onions, sliced, white and green parts separated
- 2 cloves garlic, minced
- 2 Tablespoons ginger, minced
- 3 Tablespoons red curry paste
- 2 teaspoons turmeric
- 8 cups chicken stock
- 14 ounces coconut milk
- 2 Tablespoons lime juice
- 1 1/2 pounds chicken, cooked and shredded
- 8 ounces brown rice noodles
- 1/2 cup cilantro, chopped
- Optional: Limes, more cilantro for serving

Directions

1. Heat large pot over medium heat and add coconut oil.
2. Once oil is hot, add carrots and red pepper. Season with 1/4 teaspoon salt and sauté until soft, about 5 minutes.
3. Add mushrooms and white parts of green onion. Season with 1/4 teaspoon salt and sauté until soft, about 3 minutes.
4. Add garlic and ginger, and sauté for one minute.
5. Add red curry paste and turmeric and sauté for 30 seconds.
6. Slowly pour in chicken stock, scraping browned bits from bottom of pot.
7. Stir in coconut milk and lime juice. Bring to boil then reduce to simmer. Cover with lid.
8. Allow to simmer for 30 minutes to 1 hour to develop flavor.
9. Remove lid and add chicken and noodles. Let simmer for about 5 minutes, or until noodles are al dente.
10. Right before serving, stir in cilantro and green parts of green onions.
11. Serve soup with lime wedges and more cilantro.

Slow Cooker Version

If you want to adapt this recipe for a slow cooker, simply dump all ingredients except chicken, noodles, green parts of green onions, and cilantro in slow cooker and cook on low for about 6 hours.

Once the 6 hours is up, add chicken and noodles and cook for an additional 5 to 10 minutes in the slow cooker on high, or until the noodles are al dente. Right before serving, stir in the cilantro and green parts of green onions.

Feeling overwhelmed? I understand. I have immersed myself in nutrition the past fifteen years; I have studied nutrition repeatedly for it to become my new "normal." As more people incorporate this real food eating plan, which is mostly vegetables, we will see a shift in the overall health trajectory of our population. You do not have to change everything TODAY. But, each change that you make this month and over the next few years will create a major shift in your health trajectory. Think about it this way—make a change each month for a year. At the end of the year, you have made 12 changes in your life. That is HUGE! That is a realistic way to create healthy habits. You can do this. I believe in you. And I have walked a similar path over the last 15+ years. But. You. CAN.

SEEDS SOWN

Questions to Journal

I shared an abundance of ideas and facts about nutrition. What were the top three things that intrigued you?

What two or three ideas seemed to challenge you the most?

What are or have been the three most challenging things for you to change in your nutrition choices? Why?

Are you ready to work on one? Which one? Put a star by it if you need to reach out to a mentor for support or accountability.

_____

_____

_____

_____

_____

_____

_____

_____

_____

_____

_____

CHAPTER 13

RESTORATION THROUGH EXERCISE

"Therefore, since we are surrounded by such a great cloud of witnesses, let us throw off everything that hinders and the sin that so easily entangles, and let us run with perseverance the race marked out for us. Let us fix our eyes on Jesus..."

HEBREWS 12:1-2a

The day I watched our youngest take his first steps onto the bus as a kindergartner, I started walking consistently. I knew for sure my days of having any more babies were done. Our kids were all in school, and that put my health in a new rung on my priority list. I had more time in my schedule to dedicate to exercise. We lived in a Minneapolis western suburb, and our neighborhood backed up to one of the many old railroad tracks they had converted to walking/biking/running paths. Everything was in place for regular exercise—time, safe walking location, and desire. The only obstacle was our long winters accompanied by abundant snow. I would have to work on a plan to overcome that obstacle.

I conquered that obstacle a few years later when I came up with the idea of adding a dog to be my accountability partner in my passion for walking. I had a few qualifications for this dog. It had to be big enough to walk reasonable distances. It had to be as hypoallergenic as possible for my husband and a few other family members with respiratory allergies. I had decided I was dedicated to being a good dog owner. After some online research, I decided on a medium-sized GoldenDoodle. I located a reputable breeder in Wisconsin. The next step was introducing and "selling" my idea to our family. My husband was more shocked because of the price tag; but, with some persuasion, he was on board. Our kids agreed, as long as I didn't purchase an "ankle biter." That was a pretty easy sales pitch, and I reached out to the breeder to put in our deposit for the next litter.

Andy joined our family in March of 2013, and I can honestly say we have been walking every day his whole life. After we moved to Florida, we established care at Andy's new veterinarian; he did his initial exam, looked at me, and clarified Andy's age. I smiled and reminded him that we walk, on average, 10,000 steps each day. That appointment and each of my yearly physicals confirmed the same answer. Regular exercise was benefitting both of our health journeys.

I introduced my neighbor, Jessica, earlier in this book. It is time to fully share how our friendship has enriched our health through our exercise routines; and then I will share tips, ideas, and the research that will back it all up. Exercise looks different for everyone, but regular exercise will add value to your health journey and help every part of your body.

Walking with Jessica

After I moved in, we started walking on Sunday mornings. Walking each Sunday works well for our schedules. She serves our country in one of the branches of the Armed Forces, and I have great respect for her service; and I know that on some Sundays, her service to our country comes before our routine walks.

Let me share a few details about Jessica and her level of dedication to exercise. She is multiple levels above me in the exercise world. She runs and participates in races of varying lengths and levels of difficulty. I cheer her on as running is not in my repertoire. She also is an avid strength trainer. I always love it as she shares how she can participate in training "the elite" in the branch where she serves. First, they don't always have a spot for her when she inquires about being added to their group. She shows up and "participates" on the edge of the group. After the group sees that she can keep up with them, they add her to the class. She is also many more levels higher than I am in the strength training category. You may be asking, "Why does she just walk with you on Sunday mornings?" I have asked that many times, too. It turns out that our walks on Sundays are her "rest" days. I take that as a compliment and laugh each time she shares those stories of her workouts with her military groups throughout the week.

Take note of those around you that may be a few levels ahead of you in the exercise realm. I don't ever feel intimidated by Jessica's advanced level of exercise. She inspires me every day. I love to hear her stories about how she is training for each race and what she does in her strength training groups. Thankfully, she shares her wisdom and helps me see how I can "start" with different regimens to help me in any exercise area. She understands my level and casts a vision of what I can do to level up at my pace. Her level of expertise is one of the many reasons I love her. She never pushes me. She inspires me. And I remind her that we will walk our dogs on those "cold" Florida mornings in January. We don't skip because of the "cold" in Florida; "cold" is less than 50 degrees. For all the Midwest and Northern readers, you have full permission to roll your eyes and laugh at the Floridians.

I eluded to the details that Jessica shared about our walks. She uses various apps and devices to track her fitness achievements. Jessica knows which routes around our neighborhood we can take to achieve either distance or steps. She also tracks our pace. During my chemotherapy treatment, my pace was markedly slow. She still walked with me each Sunday I had the energy to get out and walk. My treatment ended the last week of October; and as we were finishing our walk in mid-January, she looked at our stats and declared, "Your pace is back to normal!" We did a little happy dance and a high-five! That was a marker that I was ahead of schedule in the recovery period following chemotherapy. I was educated that the six months of chemotherapy came with a six-month recovery period. After that news, I declared myself ahead of schedule. Score! God provided me with ahead-of-schedule healing as well as the choices I had made nutritionally during my treatment. Together, God and whole food nutrition proved to be a great combo.

Our average walks on a Sunday morning are 6.4 miles. We walk that in about 2 hours, and our average pace is approximately 17–19 minutes, depending on how many potty breaks our dogs take. We have a good pace and chat the whole time. We have multiple neighborhoods and combinations of how we walk them to achieve our 6.4-mile goal. When we start, we tell the dogs which neighborhoods we are walking, and they know which streets to turn on. They know the routine and each cul-de-sac we walk, so we optimize our step count and distance.

There are so many benefits to having a walking friend. The first one is accountability. We will each admit that there would be some days we would think about skipping until the other one sends the text on Saturday evening to confirm the time we are walking. And we laugh as we finish our walk the following day because we are glad we didn't skip. Find your accountability partner for your exercise.

The other benefit is the chatting. We chat about everything. And these chats make us laugh; some bring us to tears, but they bring us closer together in the end. We have a "zone of privacy" around our relationship, which we hold in high honor. Because of our "zone," we know that our emotional well-being will be much better after our conversations, no matter what we discuss. I shared many emotions as I went through my chemotherapy and our walks were the best medicine.

The last benefit I want to share here about having a friend to walk with is what you learn on your walks. We are both "nerds," and I say that lovingly in our own ways. Because of that, we do a lot of reading, research, and searches online. On these walks, we share all these points of interest and then make plans about how we will put them into our lifestyle or routines. It is a big win for our overall health.

There are many more benefits to having a walking partner than I have described, but I think you get the idea of the value of an accountability partner in your exercise routine. Find your accountability partner soon and enjoy all the benefits in addition to the exercise.

Details of Consistent Exercise

*Disclaimer: Before you start any exercise, please check with your PCP.

How does exercise restore your body to health? Just as with the other areas we have discussed—nutrition, gut health, sleep, and stress—exercise helps our bodies return to homeostasis.

Exercise will impact each area of your health, but let's list out some:

- Mind – Exercise will help lower stress, and anxiety, and improve mood.
- Heart – Cardio exercise strengthens your heart muscle, lowers your blood pressure, and helps stabilize your cholesterol levels.
- Gut/GI System – Exercise helps your GI system move well and promotes better digestion and GI mobility—pooping once or more daily.
- Muscular System – Exercise will help your muscles be flexible, increase their strength, and can help improve your balance.
- Lymphatic System – A target exercise for your lymphatic system to help it work consistently. There is no "pump" in our lymphatic systems, so our

muscles and movement create the "pump" to move the contents through it.

- Respiratory – Consistent exercise will help promote better oxygenation of your body through deeper breaths as you change your pace of movement.
- Skeletal System – Regular exercise promotes strong bones.
- Sleep – General rule of thumb is that with regular exercise, you will most likely start to sleep better.

As with any of the other areas we have discussed, when you start exercising, your body notices it and starts making changes immediately to be healthier. Those changes are made at a cellular level, so we don't "see" them; but we feel the effects through more energy, better sleep, and focus. We get these "recovery" signs as soon as the first day we start to move. The more we move on a routine basis, the faster our bodies "recover" and return to a healthy state of homeostasis.

What about my numbers? Regular exercise is going to positively affect weight, blood pressure, cholesterol, and blood sugar/HgbA1C. How quickly will those numbers change? That varies for everyone; but if you walk 60 minutes each day for a month or longer, you should start seeing the changes after that. You can take your blood pressure at home once or twice a week in the morning if your BP has been on the borderline or a bit higher. Write down your findings, and you can see the trend. These findings give your PCP more information to help them make a more qualified decision in your care plan.

Cholesterol numbers can be checked at your PCP's discretion. Cholesterol numbers are not emergent for the vast majority of people. Obtaining a reading once or twice a year is generally sufficient. The consistent monitoring of your labs will be the subtle or not so subtle reminder of the impact and importance of consistent exercise.

Blood sugars for Type 2 Diabetes should steadily decrease with regular exercise. If you are changing your eating habits and exercising consistently, you should see improvements more rapidly. Your PCP or Endocrinologist will give you specific orders for managing your blood sugar assessment if they want you to check it at home and can share multiple resources for both exercise and nutrition.

What about weight? My general rule of thumb with weight and exercise is this. If you are walking 60 minutes every day, think long term. Walking each day will bring weight loss after a few months of walking. It may happen earlier, but give your body 2–3 months to see more noticeable weight loss if walking is the only change you are implementing. If you choose to do a more intense activity or cardio, you will see changes in your weight quicker. Your goal for weight loss should be 1–2 lbs. each week.

Tools to Exercise

What do you need to start exercising? Nothing. I am serious. Most people have a pair of tennis shoes to walk in. Walking is the most basic exercise you can do; and as long as you live in a safe neighborhood, all you have to do is open your door and start to walk. Do you have a bike in your garage that you haven't used in a while? Do you have bike paths or safe roads, or sidewalks to use? Start riding your bike. Don't overcomplicate exercise. Start small and basic. Do something every day.

What else can you do without spending any money? A lot. Yoga. Pilates. Strength training. The list is endless. Open up your computer, tablet, or smartphone and get online. There are so many workout videos available on the internet it can boggle your mind. And the strength trainers will teach you how to use the things you have around your home for weights, so you don't need to purchase anything. You can also use your body weight for a "weight." Again, the creativity is there to do any type of exercise without spending a dime.

What about gym memberships? That is a personal decision. Some people thrive in the gym environment, and some love the classes provided at a gym. If that is your vibe, definitely find your tribe at your local gym. There is a benefit to working out in a "team" environment.

Do you like to work out at home? That is another excellent option if you have the space. As I noted above, you don't need to add any equipment. Be creative and use what you have. As your budget allows and you know what you will use the most, purchase what you want with cash.

At-home gyms can be tailored to what you will use and the space available for the equipment you want to purchase.

Can I create or access a workout routine? Of course. Open up your preferred search engine on your internet and type in the keywords of what you want to work on specifically. You should be given a list of options. Browse through the choices. Print out a few options to compare. You can always create a unique routine based on the suggestions you see listed in the options. Engage in a great conversation with a friend or colleague of yours who is more versed in exercise/ strength training. Have a chat with them and show them what you have come up with. They can provide you with additional ideas if they have some. Having a few different options to switch things up and add variety to achieve your goals is excellent.

What about working out when I travel for my job? There are endless options for that also. Know the environment where you will be staying and make the choices that suit you. The easier you make it for yourself, the more likely you will stay committed to your choices of working out as you travel.

Goal Setting with Exercising

What is your goal? Are you more consistent if you have a race or plan to strive towards?

Tracking your Exercise:

- Do you use a device, i.e., FitBit, Garmin, AppleWatch, etc.?
- Do you use your smartphone—Google health or Apple health
- Do you use an app on your phone?

These options are great for a few reasons. Think of the devices and apps as personal online accountability partners. I am cautious to remind you not to let all of these technology options overwhelm you as you use them. Don't let them become a micromanager of your health. Track your numbers with the help of technology and use them as a guide.

The devices and apps can also help you track the positive outcomes by adding new healthy habits to your lifestyle. They also will be able to show you if you get off track a little or a lot. Use these times you are off track as learning points, and don't put yourself in detention. No one is perfect. We all slide a little. Learn and move on with better information and better choices.

Here are a few walking goals to use, or they may inspire you to create a unique one that piques your interest.

- 10,000 steps each day—this is a worthy goal to work towards to improve or maintain your health. Ten thousand steps each day is 3.6 million steps in a year.
  - If you are below that, set a goal to walk 500–1000 more steps daily for a week or two. Then increase it by 500–1000 more steps each day until you hit 10,000 steps per day.
- Would you like to walk a little more? Increase your step count each day to 14,100. This brings your yearly total to 5 million steps.
- Do you not exercise at all? Then start by walking 1 or 2 days a week. After a month, if you have more time in your schedule, add another day to your walking routine.

Exercise is not everything in achieving better health. Exercise can have an impact in many areas of your body, so it is important. You can choose what you want to do, how often, whether in a group, with a buddy, or by yourself. The main point is to move each day. Our bodies need it. It's not a fun thing to do for our bodies. It is maintenance for good health and good life. You are the captain of your exercise routine. Take the time to learn, implement, and review. Switch up your exercise routine as you want. Be creative. But move every day of your life.

Questions to Journal

Have you narrowed down where you like to exercise? If so, where is it? If not, take some time to jot down pros and cons to the gym, your neighborhood, your home, etc.?

Have you thought about finding Scripture verses that encourage you to move or exercise? Look for them, write them out, and say them aloud daily to encourage you to implement routine exercise into your life.

What is your "line-in-the-sand" reason for implementing routine exercise? Write it out. Review it periodically and add more clarity to it as additional moments of detail are generated by the Holy Spirit.

_____

_____

_____

_____

_____

_____

_____

_____

_____

_____

CHAPTER 14

RESTORATION IN SLEEP, PEACE, AND CONTENTMENT

"Peace I leave with you; my peace I give you. I do not give to you as the world gives. Do not let your hearts be troubled and do not be afraid."

JOHN 14:27

This scripture gives us total comfort. But, then again, we get distracted by all of the distractions of this world. My distraction was the diagnosis of colon cancer. And that's where the relationship with Alison impacted my journey of healing.

Renee and Alison

After moving to Florida, I quickly found a Bible Study Fellowship (BSF) class as I had attended in previous cities where we lived. As I entered the room with our small group, I saw two gals chatting. As we went around the room and shared a bit about ourselves, I soon learned that Renee was a hairstylist and

Alison was a massage therapist. I also learned they were best friends; but as I soon figured out, they were sisters from different mothers. They were inseparable. Like any woman who just relocated, I asked for their contact information; finding a great hair stylist is imperative, and a good massage therapist is an excellent bonus!

Hair Restoration is more than just a Good Cut and Color

I have been their client since we met at Bible study. If you see a picture of me, Renee gets full credit for how great my hair looks. After my surgery and confirming that my polyp was a cancerous tumor, I went for my usual cut and color with Renee. We discussed the plan of care being set up, and she asked at the end when I wanted to schedule my next appointment. I sadly looked at her and said, "They say I will be able to keep my hair, but I wasn't exactly confident of their predictions." I told her I thought we should wait to schedule an appointment after my six months of treatment. Then she could fix what was left. She hugged me and agreed. She had a plan in place already to help with any damage that might occur during my treatment. Can I get an A-MEN for all the fantastic hairstylists out there!

Through my journey, I did lose a lot of my hair. My best estimate is that I lost 80%; it became extremely thin. I still had some length to it, but it was abysmal. It was stringy and sparse. I did find some hair extensions that looked like a ponytail. I grabbed a few and found they were perfect to create the illusion of the BEST messy bun I have ever had! For most of my treatment, I worked my hair up in a messy bun with my extensions and a fun headband. It became my signature look. I did order a few scarves and would wrap them around my head some days for a different stylish look with pathetically lousy hair.

As treatment was coming to an end, I was pretty excited to make my first appointment back with Renee. She knew it was best to wait a month after treatment was finished to start the regrowth treatment and create a new style of what was left. You know your stylist is talented when you arrive at her salon, sit in her chair, and undo what is left of your messy bun, knowing you will walk out of the salon looking like a model. She assessed my hair and said with the broadest smile, "I know just what to do." I said, "Do your thing. And let's start my healing with a cute new look!"

She did her magic; and when my blowout was completed, I was stunned! I hadn't had "short" hair in many years. She styled the cutest "bob" hairstyle I have seen! Later that day on Facebook, a high school friend commented, "Ann, you have 'hot old lady hair!'" Leave it to the boys to bring you back to the reality that you are not in your twenties anymore—LOL.

My hair continues to grow steadily and thicken, too. It's another sign that our bodies want to maintain homeostasis. Even the hair on our heads returns. Our bodies are amazing. Each part returns to as close to normal as it can after receiving chemotherapy. I was devastated to lose it. But restoring my hair has provided a new peace I have never felt before. I know my hair is not what makes me, me. It is a gift to enjoy and know that however it looks as it returns will be how God has ordained this chapter of my life to be. That is one of the many facets of restoration. Finding peace with the gifts we are given, the bumps we experience, and the setbacks that throw us off course. Jesus is our peace in each situation. He promised it in the book of John, as I quoted above.

More than a Massage

Massage therapists have a wide variety of focus and knowledge. Some do it for fun; some are highly educated, and their massages make a difference in our bodies. Alison falls under the last qualification. She is wicked smart and continues to add to her learning and credentials in a steady cadence. In fact, during my chemo treatment, she texted me to see if I was available to come and be a "body demo" for her during her training in lymphatic drainage. I thought for maybe 2 seconds and replied, YES! I was going to have to lie on her massage table for about 4 hours, and she was going to learn the techniques using my body for the training. When you don't feel good and are invited to have your body "worked on," you don't delay your response. And I ended up helping her for two days. Always an avid learner, I kept my ears open as the instructor was training. I learned a lot about my lymphatic system and how each position that she was doing impacted its workings. During my surgery, I had 16 lymph nodes removed along with the left descending colon and a port implanted by my left shoulder in my subclavian vein. Both surgeries impacted how my lymph system drained and worked after. Seeing the difference between the left side of my body compared to my right side was incredible. I now support having lymphatic work done on my body on a routine basis. The more you know, the better you care for your body.

As I finished my treatment, I resumed my regular massages with Alison. My body was a wreck and needed consistent massages. Over time, we saw improvements. It is prevalent when you have a port placed for the muscles around it to be very tight. Mine were at the start of my healing journey; but over time, as Alison used her combined skills, they did start to loosen. She used differing techniques from my head to my toes to relax each part. After each session, she reviewed items to work on, especially stretching before and after I walked with my dog. She also encouraged any yoga that I would add in. I believe her comprehensive care was and continues to impact the restoration of my body. I am so thankful.

The medicines to minimize nausea and vomiting slow down your GI tract, which leads to constipation. I thought constipation would be alleviated immediately after treatment. But, the impact on my gut from the antiemetics given during chemo lasted about 6+ months after. My GI system was still sluggish even with walking and eating a good amount of fiber. Alison used some techniques that would help my system improve almost immediately. It didn't last forever, but the accumulative effect has. And now, almost daily, I do a series of yoga poses by Dr. Josh Axe, called "Gut Yoga." Google it, and the instructions for the poses will populate. This continues to be the best thing to keep my GI system in a regular rhythm.

If you have not found a massage therapist to complement your medical team, I do highly recommend it. Our bodies respond to each care team's impact. We have many systems to take care of to return to optimal health. If we leave out an area of our body for maintenance, we may have a body system that remains unhealed. And if one system is left unhealthy, the other parts will be impacted. I hope you find this information helpful as you move forward in your health journey.

Sleep, Peace and Contentment

Sleep, peace, and contentment are the steps of healing initiated as we change our mindset and continue to be worked on throughout our entire life. A solid sense of peace and contentment will impact your sleep, but this varies depending on the person.

Sleep

Many factors in our lives impact our sleep. The amount of sleep varies by person, but most people feel best if they sleep 7–8 hours at night. Knowing the amount of sleep you need is helpful, and you can work on the other things impacting achieving those hours.

One of the most common factors of sub-optimal sleeping is working the night shift or any other "off" or "swing" shift. Sleeping during daylight hours can be easy for some, but it is not normal or easy to accomplish for most. Many resources are available, and your fellow night shifters have even more tricks that work well.

Sleep for all of us can be elusive some nights, or possibly it is routine sleep problems. If you are experiencing frequent sleep problems, seek help from your PCP, a sleep specialist, a massage therapist, etc. Most importantly, refer back to the chapters on nutrition and exercise. Nutrition and exercise are the primary ways to help our bodies minimize inflammation and return to homeostasis by fueling it correctly and moving it consistently.

Can I put a plug in for quality sheets?! I am going to. I have used sheets from many companies. And after staying at a friend's condo for a weekend and sleeping better than I had for a while, I had to ask her, "What sheets do you have?" And she shared her top options for sheets they had discovered at a beautiful bed and breakfast. I ordered the sheets immediately and called my sister to do the same. Here's a tip you never thought you would receive in a book about health. I highly recommend www.comfybedsheets.com.

How old is your pillow? How old is your mattress? A new pillow and an updated mattress are my next tips. The last details or tips—what is the temperature in your room? It is suggested to lower the temperature when you sleep. I always go back to the basics in each area.

Peace and Contentment

I am not talking about world peace. That won't happen. We live in a sinful world; until Jesus returns, there will always be conflict. I am talking about the peace that Jesus describes in the scripture at the beginning of this chapter. The only peace we can have on this earth is from Jesus. And the only way that we obtain this is when the Holy Spirit opens our hearts to believe in Jesus. We don't do anything in this process. It is all up to God. If you are reading this and don't know Jesus, please keep reading, as I believe God has an exciting opportunity coming your way because you are reading this book.

How do we, as sinful people, experience peace and contentment while we are here on earth? This is a powerful question and does not have a concise answer. It will spur on some powerful, I pray, in-depth conversations. And I do encourage you to have those conversations. Don't shy away from the conversations you do not feel prepared to have. Your trepidation may be because you are unsure what to ask, or you may be on the receiving end of the question. Either way, pause and ask the Holy Spirit to guide your words. It's amazing how asking the simple question of the Holy Spirit will start that process of peace and contentment as you ask Him for help.

Peace and contentment arc a life-long process here on earth. It looks different for everyone as we each walk out our journey. A relationship with Jesus as I described throughout this book is the best way to experience peace and contentment while you live. I will encourage you yet again, to open up the Bible, go to church, and have many conversations throughout your life. Ask, seek, knock. The door of peace will be opened to you.

Questions to Journal

In what or where have you been searching for peace or contentment?

How have each of these things left you searching for the next "thing?"

Are you ready to have some conversations with others who know Jesus? Are you ready to start to ask some questions that have been too hard to ask before? Call or text a friend.

_____

_____

_____

_____

_____

_____

_____

_____

_____

_____

_____

_____

_____

CHAPTER 15

RESTORATION IN HEALING

"But the fruit of the Spirit is love, joy, peace, patience, kindness, goodness, faithfulness, gentleness, and self-control."

GALATIANS 5:22 NIV

"Restore to me the joy of your salvation and grant me a willing spirit, to sustain me. Then I will teach transgressors your ways, so that sinners will turn back to you. Deliver me from the guilt of bloodshed, O God, you who are God my Savior, and my tongue will sing of your righteousness. Open my lips, Lord, and my mouth will declare your praise."

PSALM 51:12-15 NIV

Restore

Restore is not a word that is used much, if at all, in the medical field. Our physicians tell us how our bodies will heal, which is good. When our bodies are broken or have taken ill, we desire our bodies to heal. As I started my journey, though, I desired more than healing. The longer I prayed and talked with my sister and other prayer warriors, I desired restoration. I wanted God to restore my soul, too. I longed to create a deeper relationship with Him. I wanted more than earthly healing. I was past the worldly desire for wellness we hear of each day. Restoration will be the focus of this chapter. A further, deeper, and more intimate space of healing that encompasses the whole of our created bodies—our body, mind, and soul.

Open your Bible to the Gospels. The selected miracles that are recorded have a thread woven in them. Jesus performs the miracles, but He asks those who experience them to do something. Jesus requests our action in the midst of the miracle. The actions of the recipients of the miracles are not the reason the miracle happens. But, Jesus teaches an important lesson for all of us now. Jesus shows us He will perform the miracle, but we are an active part of that miracle happening.

Here are a few examples with Scripture references:

- The woman who touched his hem and was healed, Matthew 9:18-22. Jesus healed her because of her faith in Him. BUT, her action caught his attention.
- Peter walking on water WITH Jesus, Matthew 14:22-33. Peter was fearful, but Jesus said, "Come." Peter got down out of the boat, walked on the water and came toward Jesus.
- Jesus heals a paralytic, Mark 2:1-12. Jesus said to the paralytic, "I tell you, get up, take your mat and go home." He got up, took his mat and walked out in full view of them all.
- Jesus feeds the five thousand, Mark 6:30-44. Jesus asked, "How many loaves do you have? Go and see." The disciples found out they had five loaves and two fish.

These are a few; but as you read these accounts and the others in Scripture, you will continue to see that God lets us participate in the miracle of healing. As I have shared my testimony, I have shared the things I have done. But I also have said that it was God's will and God's healing; and those two things alone restored my health. God asked me to be active in my healing journey. He asks many of us to do something.

Many times we pray and wait. Sometimes that is the correct thing to do. But when Jesus calls us to action, we need to be obedient to His call. Sometimes what He is calling us to do is action for others and their healing. But Jesus calls on each of us to take part in the restoration process. It is not our job to question, but to be obedient. Let God do the miracles; and when you are asked to be part of it, give Him the glory!

Body

Restoration of our bodies is never fully complete while we are on earth. As I said earlier, our bodies do want to maintain homeostasis. However, on earth, our bodies are constantly in a tug of war to maintain that homeostasis while fighting off the assaults of sickness and disease. We do the best we can, or we become lax and give in to the desires of our minds and stomachs. For most of us, it is a mixture of the two options throughout our lives. In most moments, we focus on helping our bodies work toward homeostasis. With possible moments of following the desires of our stomachs and our minds, the tug of war continues throughout the entirety of our lives.

The last four chapters have been written as points for each of us to follow and use as a guide; however, it is not complete. I will continue my education until I finish my earthly chapter. I hope you will, too. These chapters are an excellent foundation to help you get started. The amount of knowledge and wisdom for our health is copious. It can be overwhelming. As I have shared, we can be easily distracted by the "shiny" promises of the following option for wellness: *Be on guard as you add to your health wisdom, but search diligently for the available wisdom.*

Form a team that will challenge you in good ways. You want to gather those around you who will help you level up in the areas we have discussed. And you, too, will challenge your team as you level up alongside them. You may be surprised at who is added to your "Restoration Mastermind Group" as your life moves forward. I have been.

We all have the opportunity to add health to our bodies each day of our lives. We all have bodies with specific needs and challenges. And with both needs and challenges, we can advance our health further than we may have believed. The most awesome Creator created our bodies. We may see some crazy transformations in our life or the lives of our friends and family. And they are usually from those simple steps I described earlier—movement, nutrition, and rest. Those are the things God has provided to us from the very beginning. A simple reminder to not overcomplicate your health journey and to not miss the truth.

Mind

The mind is a wonder of creation. It is so intricately created; it will never be fully understood nor grasped.

We have all witnessed people whose minds have been controlled in ways we cannot humanly explain. But we have seen how the mind can handle each part of our body in extraordinary ways. As a nurse, I have seen things that I cannot discuss, but they have blown me away as I saw them happen. And these manifestations leave us all with a question—Why?

The restoration of our minds on earth results from God's presence in the lives and minds of people. He has given us individuals gifted to help people's minds achieve the amount of restoration God has granted. In the field of Mental Health and faith-based workers, God has planted some people with a specific gift of helping others heal/restore in this area. As I described in Chapter 11, you may search to find the correct person with the proper training and personality that resonates with you or the person who needs their guidance. They are out there, though. Ask in prayer, through conversations, and with your care providers.

Why do I confidently say that the restoration of our minds here on earth is the result of God? I have seen it personally and in many people that I know. Additionally, if medications or therapy were the solution, the side effects of our minds being a mess would not be happening. Are medications needed for our mind when it is sick? Yes, they can be beneficial, but they are not healing. They will help lessen symptoms of our mind when it is unhealthy, but no medication will completely heal a sick mind. There are good therapists who help many people uncover things that help their minds heal more, but not entirely.

Seeing God come into someone's mind and heal it is so indescribably wonderful! Many of us have seen it. It is documented in the pages of the Bible; and if you ask around in trusted relationships, they will share their testimony of God's healing.

Yet some of you also have a story you can tell where God didn't heal a person in your life. And the most fundamental question—Why?—is asked. My best answer is that some miracles are not performed on this side of heaven; some miracles are performed for believers as they run into their Savior's arms upon entering heaven. Again, this is the most complex miracle for us to embrace. On earth, we are left with the gaping hole of their absence, and having an army of prayer warriors to lift us in prayer and surround us physically when we are weak is a blessing.

You are never alone. Again, I want to remind you that God loves you and is with you right now as you read this book. Even if you don't believe in Him, He is with you. If this is something you are struggling with right now, close your eyes and let God's presence bring you peace that only He can. Take time right now to feel His presence and peace.

Soul

As created beings, our souls are an intimate part of us. God created everything by speaking them into existence on this earth and throughout the universe. He spoke everything into being EXCEPT man and woman; we were made out of the dust, and then he breathed into us. Take a moment to reflect in AWE of this; and if you are not familiar with it, read Genesis chapters one and two.

Humans are different from animals and all other created things because we have been given a soul. Because God breathed life into Adam, we can know God. Our soul is what causes us to acknowledge that there is right and wrong. Our soul is the breath of life that makes a baby cry at birth. It is also what ceases as someone takes their last breath as they pass away. We don't have control over it, but it is there. Believer and non-believer, we each have a soul.

The restoration of our soul is a work of our Father, His Son, Jesus, and the Holy Spirit. Our response to them is critical. We either say yes, we believe, or we reject their offer. By saying yes, we acknowledge their existence and then build a relationship with them. By saying no, we deny their existence and will live a life without them for eternity. I can't explain it any further than this, but I know it. As a believer, I know without a doubt Jesus is my Savior. The restoration of our souls is shared throughout the pages of the Bible. As we each study, God will reveal to us precisely the longings of our souls and fill us each with what we need in our lives. It is an intimate relationship with the Father, Son, and Holy Spirit. It is going to look different but the same for each of us.

- Who has possession of your soul?
- Is God knocking on your heart's door right now? Are you listening or aware of his promptings at this time?

Some of you will need to stop and think about these two questions. Please do. The time that you spend listening to God will have an eternal impact. Do not rush. This may be a perfect time to put the book down, put on your tennis shoes, and go for a walk. Listen for God's still, small voice.

I will again share the three things that will be the best way for you to listen when God opens your heart.

- Read the Bible.
- Go to church—more than once. Possibly attend a few different churches to find the best fit for you. Confirm that the church is Scripturally sound, which means they preach only from the Bible.
- Have conversations with those who have faith firmly planted in Jesus. They will listen to you and answer your questions; and if you request, they will help you with more resources.

A Glimpse into My Time of Restoration

On October 27, 2021, I had my last chemotherapy discontinued. I made it. Twelve treatments over six months. BEST. DAY. EVER. I didn't feel great. I didn't ring the bell. Nurse Julie looked at me and said, "Go home. Go to bed. And come back to ring the bell." And I followed her orders. I felt horrible. I was exhausted. I just wanted to sleep. I drove home, changed clothes, and crashed on the couch with my dog.

After the next few days, I felt better. Less nausea. No more cold sensitivity. My hands started to heal relatively quickly from peripheral neuropathy. I began to walk more. I was still exhausted from COVID, but I was making a comeback.

November 21, 2021, was a BIG day! It was a Sunday. At the start of our walk, I looked at Jessica and declared, "Let's do ALL of Kent!" She looked at me with shock and a huge smile. I reassured her that if I felt weak at any point, I would let her know. And off we went like two little girls in a candy store! And I made it. We walked 5.4 miles, our usual distance. The pace wasn't our average, but our distance was. Boom! 3+ weeks after chemotherapy completion, I was strong enough to be back at our average Sunday walking distance.

In early 2022 I entered my close surveillance portion following colon cancer treatment. I passed my colonoscopy with a clean and "sparkly" colon! My GI doctor laughed when I requested the "sparkly" adjective to be added when she dictated my colonoscopy report. The discharge nurse scowled at me when I asked her to take a picture of me jumping for joy before I got into my son's truck. She didn't think that was wise 20 minutes after waking up from general anesthesia. So, my son took my picture as soon as we arrived home. It is one of my favorites! (Disclaimer: I wake up very quickly from the anesthesia. Please follow your doctor's orders. As I have stated before, nurses aren't the best patients.) My first CT scan was good, but I had a few lymph nodes that were a bit bigger but within normal limits. My Oncologist ordered a follow-up CT Scan in three months that, when completed, showed ALL CLEAR! It was an encouraging start in my surveillance portion, and it answered many prayers from my team.

I have learned a lot through diagnosis, surgery, treatment, and surveillance. With each step, I have been reminded about the peace only Jesus can provide in our body, mind, and soul. I have personally asked for, experienced, and felt extremely grateful for each step. And I wasn't only thankful for the excellent news. I was grateful in the hard times, too. God never left me when I heard that I had a polyp or received a call from my surgeon about the pathology report that confirmed I had cancer. God picked me up and carried me those days and many others. That's a poignant reminder of restoration. God restores us as he brings us through the rough patches in our lives. The restoration doesn't always guarantee earthly healing. As I type this section, I have no guarantees of a long life. I am thankful for the health of today and the comfort He provides each day. I am focused on Him because I know other things will come up in my life and the lives of my family. And because of God's faithfulness, we will walk with His confidence towards our eternal life with Him.

As I type, I am less than two weeks from my 3rd CT scan this year. I am neither scared nor nervous. I know who holds my future. My mind, body, and soul are His. I know everyone's journey as a believer is different, and their level of relationship with Jesus is different. Some people know Jesus on Sundays when they are sitting in church, but their attitudes and actions may not reflect a "strong" faith in Him the rest of the week. You may know some people you call "hypocrites" because their actions don't match their testimony of faith. And still, others you notice are what is termed "strong" Christians. I want to clarify something. We are all the same Christians. We are all sinners in need of a Savior. We all are on our journey to building our relationship with Jesus. I like to remind people about a quote I heard that rings so true: "Church is not a Country Club for Saints; it's a hospital for sinners." Sometimes we "look" pretty good as Christians, but our sins make us unclean without a Savior. As I said, I am not nervous right now. But I have had some pretty rough days on this journey, as I have shared. I am not a "strong" Christian, but I am a Christian who needs her Savior every day. Without Jesus, my mind, body, and soul would not be as restored as they are. Our healthcare providers, therapy, surgery, and medicines can help heal our bodies in our health journey. But only Jesus can completely restore us and welcome us into heaven on our last earthly day.

I will never forget the first conversation I had with my friend Toni, who was a year out after her colon cancer treatment. The joy in her voice, the confidence as she poured into me how I would conquer this "step" in my life, and the reminder that she would pray and answer every question I had still "rocks me" to this day. Her conversation was one of the many contributing factors to the book you hold in your hands right now. She became an Ann cheerleader. She had pom poms, a rallying cry, and sent me a cute tank top to wear as I walked. I will never forget her kindness and complete support. And to everyone else on Team Ann, I will never forget your kindness and generosity. I have every card in a cute antique bucket on my desk that I look at and pray over frequently. The prayers you offered up for me, I now offer specifically on your behalf to God. What goes around, comes around. And it is my privilege to pray for each of you.

I may not have answered all of your questions about the restoration of mind, body, and soul; I don't have all the answers. I am continuing to learn and ask God to provide me with the wisdom I need daily to serve Him. I know two things for sure—**three nails and one breath forever changed our eternal destiny.** What does this mean? It is an easy way to remember the sacrifice of Jesus Christ and His resurrection three days later. He was crucified per Roman law on a cross with three nails—one in each hand and one through his feet. After six hours of suffering He gave up His spirit and died. He was removed from the cross and buried that day. Three days later, on Sunday, He took a breath. He rose from the dead and continues to live to this day. Those who believe in Jesus have the gift of eternal salvation because of his life, death, and resurrection.

Let me say this again—three nails and one breath forever changed our eternal destiny.

I want to close with a call to action. I want you to read this song or sing it. Whichever seems right to you. It is on YouTube if you aren't familiar with it. If you are a Christian, you have sung this in church or Bible Study Fellowship one time or many. It's a favorite of many. If you are unfamiliar with it, I am humbled to introduce it. And wherever you are on your faith journey, I pray that you will sing this until—It is well with your soul, too. Let go and let God.

To our sister in Christ, Sue White, your legacy continues through each of us whom you befriended—until we see each other again in Heaven.

It Is Well With My Soul

When peace like a river attendeth my way
When sorrows like sea billows roll
Whatever my lot, Thou hast taught me to say
It is well, it is well with my soul
It is well (it is well)
With my soul (with my soul)
It is well, it is well with my soul
Though Satan should buffet, though trials should come
Let this blest assurance control
That Christ (yes, He has) has regarded my helpless estate

And has shed His own blood for my soul

It is well (it is well)

With my soul (with my soul)

It is well, it is well with my soul

My sin, oh the bliss of this glorious thought (a thought)

My sin, not in part, but the whole (every bit, every bit, all of it)

Is nailed to the cross, and I bear it no more (yes)

Praise the Lord, praise the Lord, O my soul

It is well (it is well)

With my soul (with my soul)

It is well, it is well with my soul

Sing it as well

It is well (it is well)

With my soul (with my soul)

It is well, it is well with my soul

And Lord, haste the day when my faith shall be sight

The clouds be rolled back as a scroll

The trump shall resound, and the Lord shall descend

Even so, it is well with my soul

It is well (it is well)

With my soul (with my soul)

It is well, it is well with my soul

'Cause of You, Jesus, it is well

It is well (it is well)

With my soul (with my soul)

It is well, it is well with my soul. [1]

Benediction

May the seeds that were planted grow with deep roots,

May you grow to know our risen Savior more deeply each day,

May the peace of Jesus be felt by you always in your life.

And when you take your last breath, may the next step be into the arms of Jesus.

Go with His blessing and proclaim His truth!

RESOURCES

- "Luther's Small Catechism" by Martin Luther

DEVOTIONS

- "New Morning Mercies" by Paul David Tripp
- "Because He First Fed Us" by Anita Hinkeldey McVey
- "Wisdom from Above" by Charles Stanley
- "A Word to the Wise" by Paul Chappell
- "Living the Proverbs" by Charles Swindoll
- "In Search of Wisdom" by Joyce Meyer
- "Seeking God in the Proverbs" by Boyd Bailey
- "God's Wisdom for Navigating Life" by Timothy Keller
- "Becoming the Woman God Wants Me to Be" by Donna Partow
- "Live in Grace, Walk in Love" by Bob Goff

EXERCISE/NUTRITION

- "Grit and Grace" by Tim McGraw
- "The China Study" by T. Colin Campbell, PhD and Thomas M. Campbell, II, MD
- "The Blue Zones" by Dan Buettner
- "The Cancer Code" by Jason Fung, MD
- "The Obesity Code" by Jason Fung, MD
- "The Complete Guide to Fasting" by Jason Fung, MD with Jimmy Moore
- "52 Ways to Walk" by Annabel Streets
- "Chris Beat Cancer" by Chris Wark

COOKBOOK

- "Food That Grows" by Tanda Cook, ND and Sarah Marshall, ND
- "Nourishing Traditions" by Sally Fallon

PERSONAL IMPROVEMENT

- "On Fire" by John O'Leary
- "The Slight Edge" by Jeff Olson
- "Miracle Mindset" by JJ Virgin
- "Love is the Strongest Medicine" by Dr. Steven Eisenberg
- "In a Heartbeat" by Leigh Anne and Sean Touhy
- "What it Takes to Be #1" by Vince Lombardi
- "How to Win Friends and Influence People" by Dale Carnegie
- "Same Kind of Different as Me" by Ron Hall & Denver Moore
- "The Power of Positive Thinking" by Norman Vincent Peale
- "Grow Up!" by Dr. Frank Pittman
- "Hope in the Dark: Believing God is Good When Life is Not" by Craig Groeschel
- "The Mentor Leader" by Tony Dungy

TESTIMONIES OF FAITH DEVELOPMENT—read in the order listed

- "Glad You're Here: Two Unlikely Friends Breaking Bread and Fences" by Walker Hayes and Craig Allen Cooper
- "The Secret Thoughts of an Unlikely Convert: An English Professor's Journey into Christian Faith" by Rosaria Butterfield
- "My Life Without God" by William J Murray
- "The Case for Christ" by Lee Strobel
- "Christianity for People Who Aren't Christians" by James Emery White

MARRIAGE/PARENTING

- "What Did You Expect?" by Paul David Tripp
- "Parenting: 14 Gospel Principles That Can Radically Change Your Family" by Paul David Tripp
- "Teaching Your Children Values" by Richard Eyre and Linda Eyre

AUTHORS

- John Maxwell
- Dave Ramsey or any books he recommends
- Joyce Meyer
- Bob Goff
- Mark Batterson

WEBSITES FOR PERSONAL EVALUATION

- www.greatergood.berkeley.edu
- www.thework.com
- www.viacharacter.org

Questions to Ask Yourself to Find Your Passion

BY VY

- What skills come to you naturally?
- What makes you come alive?
- What is stopping you from your dream life?
- If you didn't have a single problem in life, what would you do?
- What are your interests?
- Which activity makes you feel like you are in the bliss zone?
- What things did you truly enjoy today?
- What does passion mean to you?
- What do you daydream about?
- What activity makes you lose track of time?
- What did you love to do as a child?
- What would you love to do on a daily basis?
- What is something you feel like you are suppressing for others?
- When you procrastinate, what do you do instead?
- What new skills do you want to learn?
- What are you really good at?
- What kind of legacy do you want to leave behind?
- How do you spend your time?
- What do you think you are born for?
- Who do you envy the most?
- What is something that makes you forget about everything?
- What is a minor change that will have a major impact in your life?
- What would you do even at free of cost?
- When do you feel a confidence surging inside you?
- What is common in the compliments you get?

- What is something that excites you but you are afraid to do?
- Who are your role models?
- What would you do differently if you had to start over your life?
- What is that one topic you can keep on talking about?
- Which day wasn't some special day but was most memorable?
- What is a topic that you can rant about non stop?
- What makes you feel super confident or like you have accomplished something great?
- What problems would you like to solve?
- What do your friends say you love too much?
- If you had no other problems, what would you do?
- If you knew you wouldn't fail, what would you do?
- What makes you feel drained and tired?
- What do you want to learn about more and more?
- What topic do you have knowledge about more than the average person?
- When you picture your future, what do you see yourself doing?
- What is one thing others have achieved that makes you feel jealous?
- If you had only one more year to live, how would you utilize that time?
- What is a long-term goal of yours that you are looking forward to achieving?
- If you can design your ideal work day, how would it be?
- What do you think your passion would be?

Revamp Your Kitchen For Your Healthier Eating Journey

AUTHOR: ANN GUSTAFSON, RN BSN

1. Evaluate the pace of increasing your healthier choices (fast–medium–slow)
   a. Fast
      i. Cardiac diagnosis—heart attack, stroke, high bp, or any other cardiac involvement
      ii. Food allergy
      iii. Diabetes
      iv. Cancer
      v. Body Mass Index >30, combined with any of the above
   b. Medium
      i. Body Mass >30 – >25, and no other chronic disease diagnosis
      ii. Training for an event—running, biking, swimming, or endurance
   c. Slow
      i. General desire to create healthier habits
2. Involve your family or ask a friend to work alongside you—put some fun into this activity.
3. Open up EACH cupboard, EMPTY, and CATEGORIZE the contents:
   a. Sweets
   b. Snacks
   c. Canned soups
   d. Canned vegetables
   e. Canned fruits and fruit juices
   f. Boxed or bagged cereals
   g. Spices
   h. Baking supplies

      i.   Baking mixes

      j.   Pasta

      k. Rice/grains/dry beans

      l.   Vegetable oils (corn, soy, canola)

4. Wash down your cupboards.

5. Throw out ALL expired food.

6. Suggested items with the following ingredients to remove and no longer purchase:

    a. High fructose corn syrup

    b. Artificial sweeteners

    c. Artificial colors

    d. Allergenic or intolerant foods (family specific)

      i.   Dairy

      ii. Gluten

      iii. Peanuts or other nuts

    e. Sugar sweetened drinks

    f. Fried foods–frozen

    g. Refined grains (high quality fiber has been removed)

    h. Refined sugar

    i. "Cream of" soups, or plan to minimize these ingredients

    j. Preservatives

    k. Processed cheese

7. Donate unopened sweets or other foods from the above list that you are committed to not purchasing again.

8. Throw out or eat opened foods that you are not going to use or purchase again. Place those items on your counter as you are not going to create space in your cupboards for them.

9. Take a moment to think and reorganize your cupboards based on your "new" variety of items that you will be shopping for and stocking your cupboards with.

What do you think your passion would be?

10. Restock your cupboards after you have "redesigned" the layout to support your new plan to eat healthier.

11. Research new recipes in new cookbooks, the various online platforms, blogs, etc.

12. Work as a family to create your top 10 or 20 favorite recipes. If any of these recipes need to be modified to a healthier version, put a star beside it.

13. Formulate some meal plans or search for them online or from friends. This may take some time, but embrace the fun as you search for some new recipes. You want to think about adding 1 new recipe each week or every other week. Do not plan to add in 30 new recipes in the first month.

14. Rule of thumb for processed foods—the ingredient list should be short, the ingredients should be recognized, and be able to pronounce their names. Do not purchase processed foods with added sugar. There are special occasion processed foods that you will possibly allow, i.e. birthday cake mix.

15. Create a new shopping list:
    a. Fresh and frozen fruits, no sugar-added syrups
    b. Fresh and frozen vegetables, no sauces
    c. Green tea
    d. Whole grains, rice, and dry legumes
    e. Pasta (GF or less refined)
    f. Flour and baking supplies
    g. Nuts that are less allergenic and high in omega-3
    h. Lean animal protein, grass-fed, local. Freshly caught ocean seafood or freshwater fish
    i. Herbs—grow your own, if possible
    j. Vegetables—grow your own, if possible

k. Eggs—If you want to have your own chickens to have fresh eggs, go for it.

l. Olive oil, coconut oil, grapeseed oil

m. Vinegar; apple cider vinegar

n. Condiments

o. Canned or boxed vegetables

p. Canned or boxed broths and soups

q. Bread, tortillas, crackers, etc

16. Organize this list and customize it to your grocery store. Search on Google or other platforms for grocery organization shopping lists that are already created. You do not want to fall back to "this is what we always buy." Creating this will help you create new shopping habits.

17. Set up your weekly food budget. Use cash or your debit card to stay within your budget.

18. Try a new grocery store or look differently at the items in your current grocery store. Shop with "new eyes" for the next few trips as you establish your new eating plan.

19. Enjoy stocking your freshly refurbished kitchen cupboards and pantry.

20. Organize your ingredients for the next 2-3 meals to aid in your food prep.

21. Sign up for a blog or two where you are finding most of your recipes to receive their newest recipes.

22. If you are a creative person, make a "menu" sign for your kitchen. Your family may enjoy this preview of their meals for the week.

23. Read some books, listen to podcasts, and watch some videos to support you as you start your journey. When you know more, you make better decisions and decrease your opportunity to slide backward.

24. Do you have some friends or coworkers who are interested in finding new recipes or trying new foods? Gather together on a cadence that

What do you think your passion would be?

fits your schedules to learn together and swap recipes that have been adopted as "new" family favorites.

25. Make a list of "food vacations" and write them in your calendar…these are days when there are no guidelines. These may include immediate family birthdays, holidays, vacations, Super Bowl Sunday, etc. Keep in mind that you want to eat 80% healthy meals and 20% food vacations. Mapping it out is helpful and then when you are tempted you can remind yourself of the upcoming days that are your real "vacations."

    a. 80/20 = 21 meals/week, 4 of them can be termed food vacation meals.

26. You may want to learn how to freeze or can fruits and vegetables.

27. You may find that you want to take a cooking class, or you will find many chefs have cooking videos available online.

REFERENCES

Chapter 4

1. Studies in the sermon on the Mount. Lloyd-Jones, D. Martyn. 1960

Chapter 5

1. Girl Just Pray Ministries. ™. Tykenia Mercedes
2. Ylvisaker, John Carl. "I Was There to Hear Your Borning Cry." 1985

Chapter 6

1. Time.com. "9 Questions Your Doctor Wishes You'd Ask." //time. com/4433153/9-questions-ask-doctor/
2. Cleveland Clinic. "Questions to Ask Your Doctor." my.clevelandclinic. org/patients/information/questions-to-ask-your-doctor
3. USNews.com. "21 Questions Doctors Wish Their Patients Would Ask." //health.usnews.com/conditions/slideshows/questions-doctors-wish-their-patients-would-ask
4. Square One Healing Cancer Coaching Program. "20 Questions for Your Oncologist." //squareone.chrisbeatcancer.com/twenty-questions

Chapter 7

1. Ken, Thomas. "The Doxology." 1674.
2. Bethel Music, Jonathan David Helser, and Melissa Helser. "Raise A Hallelujah." Victory. 2019. www.youtube.com/watch?v=awkO61T6i0k

3. Circle maker. Batterson, M. - Zondervan - 2016

4. Parker, Danita. "Mother's Day Prayer." May 8, 2022

Chapter 10

1. Bethel Music, Jonathan David Helser, and Melissa Helser. "Raise A Hallelujah." Victory. 2019. www.youtube.com/watch?v=awkO61T6i0k

2. Mayo Clinic. Patient Care & Health Information—Diseases and Conditions: Cancer. www.mayoclinic.org/diseases-conditions/cancer/symptoms-causes/syc-20370588

3. The Holy Bible. Exodus 20:3-17. King James Version.

4. National Geographic. "How Many Cells Are In Your Body?" Zimmer, Carl. www.nationalgeographic.com/science/article/how-many-cells-are-in-your-body

5. New Morning Mercies. Tripp, Paul David. Crossway Books. 2021. Reading for July 8.

Chapter 11

1. Oxford Dictionary of English. Oxford University Press. 2005

2. New Morning Mercies. Tripp, Paul David. Crossway Books. 2021. Reading for June 15.

3. Live in Grace, Walk in Love: a 365-day journey. Goff, Bob. Nelson Books, an imprint of Thomas Nelson. 2019. Reading for June 16.

4. Parker, Kurt. "Your Life Depends On This." July 10, 2022 Sermon.

Chapter 12

1. Harvard Health Publishing. Can Gut Bacteria Improve Your Health? October 14, 2016. www.health.harvard.edu/staying-healthy/can-gut-bacteria-improve-your-health

2. Korean Science. MINI-REVIEW. "Cruciferous Vegetables: Dietary Phytochemicals for Cancer Prevention." Razis, Ahmad Faizal Abdull. Noor, Noramaliza Mohd. www.koreascience.or.kr/article/JAKO201321365237666.pdf

3. Harvard T.H. Chan School of Public Health—The Nutrition Source. "What Should I Eat? Protein." www.hsph.harvard.edu/nutritionsource/what-should-you-eat/protein

4. American Society for Nutrition. "Protein Quantity and Source, Fasting-Mimicking Diets, and Longevity." Brandhorst, S. And Longo, V.D. *Advances in Nutrition*, Volume 10, Issue Supplement_4, November 2019, Pages S340–S350. doi.org/10.1093/advances/nmz079

5. Medline Plus Medical Encyclopedia. "Healthy Food Trends—Beans and Legumes." medlineplus.gov/ency/patientinstructions/000726.htm#:~:text=Beans%20and%20legumes%20contain%20antioxidants,help%20to%20prevent%20digestive%20cancers.&text=Legumes%20can%20be%20added%20to,be%20eaten%20warm%20or%20cold.

6. MayoClinic.org. "Healthy Lifestyle—Nutrition and Healthy Eating: Beans and Other Legumes – Cooking tips." www.mayoclinic.org/healthy-lifestyle/nutrition-and-healthy-eating/in-depth/legumes/art-20044278

7. National Library of Medicine—National Center for Biotechnology Information. "Legumes: Health Benefits and Culinary Approaches to Increase Intake." Polak, Rani. Phillips, Edward M. Campbell, Amy. www.ncbi.nlm.nih.gov/pmc/articles/PMC4608274

8. Ibid.

9. American Heart Association. "2019 ACC/AHA Guideline on the Primary Prevention of Cardiovascular Disease: A Report of the American College of Cardiology/American Heart Association Task Force on Clinical Practice Guidelines." Circulation. Volume 140,

Issue 11, 10 September 2019; Pages e596-e646. www.ahajournals.org/doi/10.1161/CIR.0000000000000678

10. IBP/Anti-Inflammatory Lifestyle P. 58, Sally Fisher, MD, MS

11. American Society for Nutrition. "Protein Quantity and Source, Fasting-Mimicking Diets, and Longevity." Brandhorst, S. And Longo, V.D. *Advances in Nutrition*, Volume 10, Issue Supplement_4, November 2019, Pages S340–S350, doi.org/10.1093/advances/nmz079

12. Northwestern Medicine—Healthbeat: Nutrition. "What Are Added Sugars? Plus How They Affect Your Body." www.nm.org/healthbeat/healthy-tips/nutrition/more-sugar-more-problems

13. Ibid.

14. New England Journal of Medicine. "Effects of Intermittent Fasting on Health, Aging, and Disease ." deCabo, Rafael. Mattson, Mark P. 2019 Dec 26;381(26):2541-2551. doi: 10.1056/NEJMra1905136. From the Translational Gerontology Branch. //pubmed.ncbi.nlm.nih.gov/31881139

15. Kylee's Kitchen Flu-Fighting Soup. www.kyleeskitchenblog.com.

Chapter 15

1. Spafford, Horatio. Bliss, Paul David. "It Is Well With My Soul." Sovereign Grace Music, Bob Kauflin

Resources

1. Vibe Inspire—Personal Development. "Find your passion with these 45 questions." vibeinspire.wordpress.com/2021/09/15/find-your-passion-with-these-45-questions. vibeinspireblog@gmail.com

ACKNOWLEDGMENTS

I want to thank the team that has been with me through the thick and thin happenings of this journey!

To my Favorite Husband, Art, Thank you for understanding all those evenings you looked over at me with my computer always in front of me as I typed this book into creation. You cheered me on, understood when I needed to take some extra walks to clear my thoughts, and believed in me from the very beginning. You are forever my FAVORITE!

To our children: Alex, Amelia (Mia), and Aaron. You have lived, loved, and grown exponentially through this journey. Your dad and I are so proud of everything you did to support me when I was journeying through cancer treatment.

To Alex and my niece, Elise: you were the two who read an early version of this book, and you didn't laugh at me. You both gently said, "find your focus." Your quiet feedback helped me have the courage to search deeper and be authentic. I am forever thankful for your faith in my ability to be a good author.

To my parents: Thank you for sharing your faith in everything you did and showing me a life based on faith in Christ is a firm foundation. Because of this, my relationship with Jesus was so natural to develop in my life. You are the main reason this book is based on faith.

To Jim and Susie: thank you for nudging me to write this book and for all of the life experiences we have had that brought us here.

To my brother Rick: you quickly took a few pictures as our dad was finishing his last harvest. Thank you for letting me use your photo on my book cover; it captured and inspired my book. We spent many hours as a family in those fields from springtime planting, through the summer days of walking beans and baling hay, and ultimately the days/evening of each harvest. You caught the soul of farming in that photo.

To Rick, Shelley, Dan, Kim, Jim, and Susie. I am the little sister in the family. You may not realize how much I have looked up to, learned from you, and wanted to live up to your wisdom through the years. Thanks for being amazing siblings and mentoring me in all ways! Love you!

To Two Penny Publishing: you listened to my idea of sharing my story. I wasn't sure how to start, but you held my hand and helped me bring an idea to a real book. I am speechless that you took a chance on me! Your team is phenomenal!!

To all of the nurses and doctors that I have worked with through the years. Each one of you has taught me, mentored me, and sharpened me to be better than the day before.

To all of my BSF friends…all the discussions as we have studied the Bible together have created a layer in my faith that I didn't realize was missing. Thank you for being the "iron that sharpens iron" in my life.

To my surgeon. You became a mentor to me in the few short appointments I had with you. Not exactly what I was anticipating when I made an appointment to have surgery. You may not have anticipated the title of mentor in my life. You said some very unexpected and important things each time we met. It all started with "Disease doesn't follow the rules." And after that, I listened a lot more closely each time you talked. Thanks again for taking care of me in the worst storm of my life.

ABOUT THE AUTHOR

ANN E. GUSTAFSON

Ann Gustafson is a daughter of the Most High King. She is a Priest in His kingdom. On this earth, she has been called to be a daughter, and a sister. She is a wife to Art, a mom to three grown children. She has been a nurse for all of her professional life, and is now adding author to her gifts from God. Ann enjoys  cooking, gardening, walking Andy every day, and connecting with her family and friends. In all these things she has been called to share His Gospel.

Made in the USA
Monee, IL
09 February 2023

27309346R00136